YOU'RE IN CHARGE...
What Now?

Other Books by Gerry Czarnecki

Take Two And Call Me in the Morning: Prescriptions for a
Leadership Headache Pain-Free for 30 days

Leadership Is Just One Thing After Another

Lead With Love: 10 Principles Every Leader Needs to Maximize
Potential and Achieve Peak Performance

Success Principles for Leaders: 7 Steps on How to Lead with Love

Work Leaders: Seven Steps For Peak Performance Leaders

You're A Non-Profit Director...What Now?

You're In Charge...
What Now?

TEN ESSENTIAL STEPS
for the Work Leader's Success

GERRY CZARNECKI

National Leadership Institute Press

You're In Charge...What Now?
Ten Essential Steps for the Work Leader's Success

Softcover ISBN-10: 1932430105
Softcover ISBN-13: 978-1-932430-10-3

Manufactured in the United States of America

Editor:	Barbara Bendall
Cover Design:	Barbara Bendall
Book Design:	Barbara Bendall
Publisher	National Leadership Institute Press

To my wife and life partner Lois,
who has been my shelter from the storms of failure
and my source of equilibrium in the sunshine of success.

You're in Charge...What Now?

CONTENTS

It's as Simple as
L-E-A-D-E-R-S-H-I-P

This book is for the more than ninety-five percent of all business leaders today directly leading employees whose work produces the results. I refer to them as *Work Leaders* because they not only *lead* others to *work,* but also actually do the work themselves.

They're the *first-level* leaders, in charge of as few as one employee or as many as twenty, who focus on achieving goals, while inspiring and energizing each of the employees directly under them to achieve peak performance results.

If you're like most people, you began your business career as someone who did the actual work, whether you were an accountant, teacher, salesperson, lawyer, engineer, research scientist or even the legendary "mail room clerk." You were assigned a set of duties which required you to create something.

But, at some point, you became so good at your job that someone decided to put you in charge of other people doing the same tasks. Suddenly, maybe overnight, you became a manager or supervisor—a Work Leader—someone who possibly:

- is a lead detective on a team investigating a homicide;
- manages a production line in an automobile plant which assembles 100 units a day;
- leads a team of colleagues on a strategy consulting engagement for a Fortune 500 company;
- manages clerks who are responsible for processing accounts receivable payments;
- leads a team of doctors treating patients in an emergency room;
- owns and manages a lawn-care service with a crew of seven;

- manages an information technology project with ten analysts;
- heads a product management team of five assistants at a Fortune 100 company;
- manages a retail store with nine sales clerks and needs to sell $250,000 of merchandise per month for the store to make money;
- leads a three-person sales team which needs ten closes a week to make the month's sales goals;
- leads a team of engineers working on the development of a component for a new-generation aircraft at a Fortune 50 company;
- runs a not-for-profit organization with a budget of $1 million and a staff of five employees who deliver services to the local community;
- owns, manages and styles hair in a salon with $200,000 a year in revenue;
- supervises a team of accountants auditing a number of public companies.

Whatever your job, as a Work Leader, you're the first level of management, what some call a "working supervisor." You manage the process, but you're also part of that process. You're a leader.

"Manager" and "leader" aren't separate categories, though some try to divide them.

"Many writers on leadership take considerable pains to distinguish between leaders and managers," wrote the late John William Gardner, an insightful author, statesman and intellectual. Gardner, who was a university psychology professor, president of the Carnegie Foundation, U.S. Secretary of Health, Education and Welfare and also served on the boards of Time, Shell Oil and American Airlines, added, "In the process leaders generally end up looking like a cross between Napoleon and the Pied Piper, and managers like unimaginative clods. This troubles me... Every time I encounter utterly first-class managers they turn out to have quite a lot of the leader in them."[1]

Gardner actually understates the point. Leadership's as important at the first level of management as it is at the top level, maybe even more so. It's impossible for a *successful* manager (note the key word *successful*) to be a bad leader because people won't continue to achieve for a failed leader.

If you've recently been put in a leadership position, you might be feeling a bit unprepared for your new responsibilities. Up until now, you've only had to concentrate on your own peak performance. You may have been helping your fellow associates with their work, but your primary assigned tasks only concerned you as an individual. Your success was *your* success, but your failure was also yours. Those were simpler times.

No doubt, you're glad to have the promotion into a leadership role, but now there are weightier responsibilities and you're the one who's accountable for them. As a Work Leader you're now expected to do a new kind of job—leading others. Perhaps you took the new leadership or management position because you liked the idea of being in charge or because you knew it was the only way to achieve the kind of success you're seeking. Maybe you thought the person who formerly held that job didn't measure up and you could do a better job.

Whatever the reason for you becoming a Work Leader, somebody decided you could do the job. Now that you're in that position, you're the one who's going to be held accountable for the peak performance results of *others*. You have to find ways to accomplish that.

Whoever the decision-maker was who decided to promote you, he or she made judgments about your knowledge, skills and attitudes. Probably that person concluded you'd succeed, but, make no mistake about it, you may also have been put into the job because you were the only person readily available. That may offend your ego, but it's often true.

Realize that as a unit leader, your success is now tied to the success of the one who put you in that position. If you fail, they fail. If they fail, you fail.

Knowing Leadership Skills Doesn't Guarantee You Have Them
Most management training programs focus on the mechanics of managing projects or processes. That's important, but there's more to it. Many managers have had those skills and still failed at their jobs. Just because you're a student of traditional leadership skills doesn't mean you know how to lead people.

"Despite the many books on management published in recent years, the MBA factories continue to turn out graduates woefully deficient in leadership insights, skills, and hands-on tools," wrote the management guru Joe D. Batten, who was founder and president of Batten, Batten, Hudson and Swab. "Taking refuge behind reams of data is still appallingly common, but it is no substitute for true leadership.[2]

Many authors have tried to define leadership, but I think the best one, loosely based on statesman and author John W. Gardner's definition, is that it's the process of successfully persuading a group to pursue the leader's objectives and goals.

You don't have to lead a country as a president or prime minister. You don't have to be a chief executive officer. You're a Work Leader who, with your team, is creating peak performance for others.

A Work Leader Is Different From a Top Leader

Most of us are fascinated with great leaders and the stories of their triumphs. However, the problem with using corporate, national or sports leaders as our role models is the world they operate in is much larger than a Work Leader's world. Most working managers and leaders simply can't realistically relate to famous leaders who make their way into news and the history books. Those people are too far removed from the daily grind of a Work Leader's job.

Someone running a branch office with a budget of less than $1 million isn't on the same level as: the mayor of a large city making a strategic decision on when to deploy a police force in a crisis; a governor deciding to reduce the size of a $20 billion budget; or a CEO increasing the profits of a $30 billion company.

Knowing Vince Lombardi shouted at each of his football players when they did something stupid on the playing field or that he created a new alignment which helped set his defenses apart in the National Football League has very little meaning to the director of a not-for-profit who needs to increase fundraising in order to avoid a deficit for the year. He's not going to accomplish too much if he screams at his employees or donors all the time.

Learning how the president of the United States uses his cabinet to decide how to deal with a crisis in a Third World country offers very little help to a first-level supervisor in the State Department who has a performance problem with her team of analysts.

Many of these well-known leaders of large organizations succeed because they hire great people, then get out of their way. This concept is often touted as the key to a leader's success and, indeed, for many at the top of very large organizations, that's a critical skill. But for real-world Work Leaders that advice could be a disaster.

An organization's results depend on strategy and execution. Organizations must do the right tasks, but they must do them the right way. Strategy sets the course for doing the right tasks, but it's execution which gets them done. That's where you come in.

"People don't work day-to-day in the big picture. They work in the nitty-gritty details of their company and its business," wrote Stanford University business professors James C. Collins and Jerry I. Porras in their book *Built to Last: Successful Habits of Visionary Companies.* "Not that the big picture is irrelevant, but it's the little things that make a big impression, that send powerful signals."[3]

The roles of a CEO and a Work Leader are strikingly different. Top executives set the course, but it's the Work Leaders who execute the CEO's plan and produce what's needed.

As a Work Leader you may delegate tasks, but you don't delegate leadership. You're a hands-on leader who must be there every day to help your staff complete the work. You have daily deadlines and expectations to meet. It's a world of task-focused activity and, as a Work Leader, you can't walk away from those responsibilities. You can't simply hire great people and get out of their way. That might work for the CEO of a large company, but not for a Work Leader who has to meet a production deadline, even though the power was interrupted for four hours.

As a Work Leader you not only need to possess leadership skills, to be active, hands-on and fully engaged in order to get your staff to respond and to deliver peak performance, but you also have to do some of the work yourself. You're getting the work done through others, but you're working, too.

You have two tasks: leadership and administration.

Leadership means you help employees under you achieve your organization's objectives.

Administration means you're actively doing tasks like: filling out employment forms for new employees, turning in timecards for payroll, filling out budgets for accounting, ordering supplies, preparing reports to other managers, communicating with customers, checking production reports and paying taxes.

As a Work Leader, you can successfully make a huge difference in your organization. You're a single individual, but you're the one putting into action the vision from the top executives. You're the one making it all happen. You're achieving your organization's goals.

Writing This Book

Most books on leadership don't focus on those who actually lead their employees and do the work. This one does. I've written *You're In Charge...What Now?* to help you do your work.

By simplifying the role of a leader into ten essential steps, I've gotten rid of everything which doesn't apply to the first level of management and leadership. Instead, I've focused on the key elements which make every Work Leader a great leader.

For this second edition, I've expanded my initial seven principles based on the mnemonic LEADER into ten principles now based on LEADERSHIP. Nothing I focused on before is lost, but I've added some core principles I believe round out a great leader.

Drawing on my life experiences from two stints in the military, a journey through academia and public speaking, as well as many years rising through the ranks of the corporate world into management, ultimately leading to entrepreneurship and the seats on numerous corporate and non-profit boards, I've condensed everything into these ten core principles.

Even if you're not a Work Leader, I think you'll find these principles still apply to you. After the first edition came out, many higher-ranked executives told me they'd forgotten the importance of these core behaviors as they moved up the organizational ranks. Unfortunately, many had failed to apply them as they became more strategic and high level in their roles, but they found that by going back to these principles, they've become even better leaders.

This book is a primer on what great Work Leaders *do,* not who they *are.* A Work Leader gets the work done, day in and day out. I know many authors focus on personality traits to define great leaders. They frequently mention words such as: "charismatic," "trustworthy" and "honest." But instead of those personality traits, I've focused on what good leaders *do*—the *actions* they take in order to make them and their organizations successful.

"What a manager/leader does on a minute-by-minute, hour-by-hour basis rarely fits any stereotype of manager, heroic leader, or executive," says Dr. John P. Kotter, an entrepreneur and Harvard University professor, "a fact that can create considerable confusion for those in managerial jobs, especially newcomers."[4]

To be a great leader, you need to work at these ten key activities every day. There are no days off. Leadership is a full-time job and requires a complete commitment to these actions—not just believing in them, but doing them every day.

The great news is if you execute these essential LEADERSHIP steps, you'll have a high probability of success. If you don't, you'll substantially increase your chance for failure. Each step relies on all the others. They may sound like simple concepts, but you have to do more than read them—you have to apply them.

As a Work Leader you need guidance and that's what this book is designed to provide. It's a handbook for your success. Think about each point, then apply it to your life and work. Each chapter has Work Leader tips and at the end of each chapter, you'll find a real-life situation case study which could happen to almost anybody. I encourage you to discuss each one with a small group of your peers. Try some role-playing to determine how you would have handled the situation differently.

I've also included a supplemental reading list for each chapter if you want to go more in-depth. Never stop learning.

As a Work Leader, you're the hands-on person leading your associates. Put these ten essential steps of LEADERSHIP into practice and peak performance can be yours.

chapter one

LOVE
A Priority for Leaders

I don't have a soft reputation. I was a "tough guy," a captain in the U.S. Army when it wasn't popular to be in the armed forces—during the Vietnam War.

After I left the military and joined the civilian work force, I rose through the ranks into leadership and became the guy who fired people. That's because throughout much of my career I was what's known as a "change agent," someone who does whatever it takes to fix broken and dysfunctional organizations. Many times that meant giving pink slips to employees, sacrificing some for the sake of the organization's health.

Yet people who have worked closely with me over the years know love is what drives my actions.

Most leaders will rankle at the word "love," thinking if they adopt that philosophy, they'll become weak and ineffective. Nothing could be further from the truth. Any leader trying to consistently achieve results and peak performance has to begin by showing love.

Friends Like, But Leaders Love

Everything a leader does begins with a capacity and commitment to love.

This idea may be disorienting, especially if you're thinking of the kind of love the Greeks called *eros,* what we call sexual or erotic love. Obviously, *eros* isn't the type of love Work Leaders should practice. Inappropriate sexual relationships with a coworker—or worse, a subordinate—hold the potential for tragedy for all concerned.

The Greeks also used the word *philia*, which defined another type of love—the love we have for family. When William Penn first settled in the New World, he named his first and most important city Philadelphia, "the city of brotherly love," where he dreamed people would treat each other as brothers.

The concept of brotherly love, or love of family, is a warm and sensitive type of love. It avoids the erotic or sexual aspects of *eros*, but goes well beyond friendship. The Greeks and much of Western civilization believed the bond between family members far exceeded that of any other relationship. Most would agree our relationships with our family members are strong and critical elements of our own personal development.

This type of unconditional love has great emotional and spiritual appeal. Unfortunately, leaders can't be this emotionally tied to their employees. In many ways, the unconditional nature of this type of love can be detrimental to a Work Leader.

That's because as a leader you have a responsibility to be judgmental. You have a duty to your group and to your superiors to achieve goals, whether you're a priest with a congregation, a supervisor with a clerical processing section, an account executive managing a client relationship, a council member representing your constituents in a city government or a team leader developing a dramatic new software program for NASA.

As good as unconditional love may feel in any of those settings, any team member not pulling in the same direction is a potential risk to your company's objectives.

You have to be prepared to focus on achievement, but if your affection is too strong for a particular employee, you'll be blinded to his or her faults. That tunnel vision may prevent you from taking the steps you need to make in order to remain on course to your goals.

The Proper Love for Your Employees

If your affection is a parental "unconditional love," or even "brotherly" love, for one of your employees who's not doing his or her job, it can prevent you from doing *your* job. If an employee isn't pulling in the same direction as the rest of the team, he or she could keep your entire group from achieving its objectives.

You can't offer the same kind of "unconditional love" parents give their children, nor can you be emotionally tied to those you supervise. So how does love factor into the equation when you have a responsibility to be judgmental of your employees as you deal with the challenges which crop up each day?

There is a kind of love you, as a Work Leader, should have toward your employees. It's the kind of love which: causes philanthropists to give vast sums to charity; leads people to help those affected by disasters; drives activists to support elimination of the death penalty; and inspires caring people to volunteer in Third World countries.

That love is expressed through a third Greek word—*agape.* That kind of love is altruistic and unselfish, sensitive to and aware of others' needs, feelings and difficulties, yet strong enough to be rational, clear-headed, non-emotional and unbiased when it comes to making decisions. It's the kind of love which inspires you to give to society and help others in need, to pay attention to them, to help them even when they find accepting help difficult, to even tell them bad news with sensitivity instead of being brutally frank and blunt.

In short, it means being sensitive to their needs, feelings and difficulties. That kind of love is an action, not an emotion. It's what you do, not what you feel.

Your employees won't listen to you or effectively follow you as a Work Leader unless they know you care about them. You have to take action to show you love them.

"Effective leaders know that you first have to touch people's hearts before you ask them for a hand," writes leadership author John C. Maxwell in his book *The 21 Irrefutable Laws of Leadership.* "That is the Law of Connection. All great communicators recognize this truth and act on it almost instinctively. You can't move people to action unless you first move them with emotion. The heart comes before the head."[5]

Organizations, no matter how technical, mechanical or structured, are comprised of people working together to accomplish a mission or a goal. Take away the employees and you don't have an organization. You're only left with ideas, theories and dreams—and that's not much.

It's only when people are working together, using the resources of science, technology, real estate and machines that goals are achieved. Human beings are the glue and brains, using capital and entrepreneurship to create results, goods and services. Without people there would be no goals.

When you understand that, your role of Work Leader becomes more clear. You're the leader who assembles employees and organizes them with available resources to get the job done. You have to be focused on your organization's progress toward and achievement of goals and objectives.

Aloha

Hawaiians have a unique culture, a deep sense of community and a strong commitment to extended family. That's all beautifully expressed in a single word of their native language—*aloha.*

Today, most visitors to the Hawaiian islands know the common use of the word. In greetings it means "hello" and "goodbye," but the true meaning of the word is "love." When a Hawaiian says, "*Aloha,*" he means, "I extend my sense and emotion of love to you." If you're arriving, it means, "Welcome with love." If you're leaving, it means, "Go with love."

The Hawaiian people express their culture as the "*Aloha* Spirit," which means, "I will live in and among my society with my fellow citizens with a spirit of love."

That's the true meaning of love for Hawaiians. To live in love is to live at peace with yourself and nature.

That's also the essence of the first principle of leadership.

Why Not Like Instead of Love?

So why use the word *love* instead of *like*? Why not say a leader must *like* people? Because when you like someone, you're thinking with your emotions and feelings instead of your head.

"Like" means you're drawn to someone's personality, core beliefs, character traits or even looks. The person may have treated you nicely, smiled at you on a day you were unhappy, complimented you when you needed confidence building, or helped you think through a personal or business problem. You may have an unexplained bond with that person which makes you feel an emotional attraction almost immediately. You feel comfortable being around that person, even if you have nothing in common with them.

Liking your associates can certainly help you enjoy the people you lead. And, since "chemistry" usually goes both ways, if you like and feel good about the people you're leading, they'll probably like and feel good about you.

So why is it wrong to like the people you lead? Because you won't like everyone and you'll be biased. You'll be somewhat against the employees you don't like—while favoring those you do like.

Very few people like everybody in the group they're leading. If you decide to be the leader of only those you like so you won't be challenged by any conflict, you'll start favoring the ones you like. In many cases, you'll look past the weaknesses of those you like, while becoming highly critical of those you don't like. You've now fallen into the trap of favorites or "teacher's pets."

Let's say you're a manager who takes over a sales force of ten, but there's one person in the group you don't like. Let's say she's also your top salesperson, with the highest customer loyalty, the best relationship with the manufacturing division and the highest peer group ratings. She's a great employee.

Rationally, you'd think you would like someone like that. But maybe her personality just rubs you the wrong way. Even though she's a top performer, you don't like being around her. If you've been a Work Leader for any period of time, you've probably found yourself in that situation and struggled with the consequences.

If liking is a requirement of good leadership, how can you lead this person? By that definition, you can't.

So what do you do?

Your dislike may become a barrier to communication with that person because you'll probably find it's difficult to hide your dislike. That leads to the other person picking up on your negative feelings. When that happens, they'll begin to react negatively toward you as well. Slowly, the two of you begin to distance yourselves from each other in an effort to avoid hostile attitudes and unpleasant encounters. As the rift between you grows, you'll probably start becoming overly critical of the person.

What's the end result?

Your hostility and bias will affect your decision making. Eventually, the tensions between the two of you may end up in you firing, laying off or transferring your subordinate.

Even though your intentions may have started out honorably,

you'll soon find when you've purged your staff of all those you don't like, you're left only with a team of people you like.

So what's wrong with that?

Because all those members you like, who now make up your team, may not be the best employees. There may be quite a few charming slackers in the group, maybe some of the friendliest people in the world who have no clue how to do their jobs, even a few buddy-buddies with sticky fingers who are pilfering from the company till or stealing credit cards from the purses of their fellow employees.

You may luck out and find your team of "likeables" ends up as a good team, but it's more likely that won't be the case.

You could argue nothing destroys a team more than a person who doesn't fit in—and that may be true. One rotten apple can indeed spoil the basket. But what if the rotten apple is one of the people you like? Doesn't that make the problem more complex and sometimes painful? This is especially true if the friend has come to believe his or her relationship with you is more important than the leadership relationship. What if they start believing their friendship with the boss is their "get out of jail free" card? They may start acting as if they can do whatever they want, slack off whenever they want, and they're protected from any consequences because they've, basically, got you in their hip pocket.

Can you discipline or fire that good friend if necessary or will your friendship prevent you from doing your job the way it needs to be done? Will you hesitate to put your company and your work first for fear you may damage your personal relationship with a member of your team? Because you like them, your bias will win.

Do you see how complicated it can get?

Remember, as a Work Leader your primary mission is to drive peak performance, not have a team of people you enjoy personally. They may make going to work fun, but they may also create serious conflicts for you when they fail to achieve peak performance. Unfortunately, when this condition exists, leaders have a tendency to ignore the problem until the entire basket is rotten. Bias wins.

Liking your employees can blind you to their weaknesses which are causing damage to your organization. That's a big problem.

We all have a tendency to overlook or even ignore weaknesses in people we like, while at the same time inflating their strengths far beyond what they really are.

Are you beginning to see what a problem that can be in the workplace? Liking your employees prevents you from seeing who they really are and blocks you from being objective about their performance.

Remember, as a leader you're accountable to yourself, your organization and, in most cases, your superiors. If liking blinds you to who a person really is, you won't be able to honestly evaluate his or her individual performance, or even that of the group. You'll let shortfalls in performance or failure to achieve goals slip through the cracks as

Work Leader's **Tip:** Avoid the Liking Trap

- You probably don't like at least one person who works for you. Make three lists: (1) all the qualities you don't like about that person; (2) all the good qualities of the same person; (3) the person's primary duties and objectives. Now evaluate that person's performance against their objectives.
- Pick the one person you like best in your work unit and make the same three lists for the same performance evaluation.
- Now compare the two sets of lists and evaluations. Answer this question: which person is the better performer and why?
- You probably have several people who work for you whom you like. Are any of them friends of yours? How long have they been friends? Do you socialize with them? How did you get to be the boss of the unit? Did you work in that unit alongside your friends or did you come from outside the work unit? How do you feel about being your friends' boss? How do they feel about it? What would you change, if anything, about your unit and the staffing? What will you change in how you're managing the unit and the people you like?
- Have you ever fired a friend? Have you ever had a friend fire you? Are you still friends? What did you learn from the experience?

you ignore, or worse fail to see, glaring problems.

When problems arise with your team, you're the one who's accountable. Are you going to blame the team's failure on external factors when it's really you and your employees who have failed to do your jobs? Are you going to let bias win?

Now let's look at it from another angle. What if you have a team of people who don't like each other. What do you do?

You get them to love each other (and I don't mean in an "office affair" kind of way, which creates a whole other set of problems).

Employees have to learn to love each other, even if they don't like other members of their team. That sense of caring is crucial to team success. You don't need to like someone to work together to achieve a goal and do the work necessary for success.

You need love—realistic, eyes-wide-open, accepting-differences, willing-to-disagree-or-discipline, don't-care-if-you-like-me, admire-the-way-you-do-your-job kind of love.

Can you feel love and warmth toward your employees, even if you don't like them? Are you patient and kind with them when you need to be and tough when the situation warrants it?

If you don't have those leadership qualities, you need to learn how to acquire them. Your team will be better for it.

"It is easy to discern those companies where warmth in management has caught on," writes sociologist, author and executive search consultant Allan Cox in his book *The Making of an Achiever.* "From first contact with the headquarters receptionist to the head of custodial services in an outlying plant, a visitor who walks the halls of a warm company and chats with its people, senses the team-play and pride that pervade its atmosphere."[6]

Back to Love

The contrast between "like" and "love" is striking and critical. You can love people, but not like them. No one's capable of liking everybody, but we can love everybody. As a leader, you must be able to care for all members of your group, whether you like them or not. Only in that way can you give your associates the commitment of truth, unbiased behavior and help they need to achieve their goals.

Effective leaders have a strong ability to communicate how much they care for the employees they're leading. Group members must perceive they're being loved. Vince Lombardi, like many great football coaches, was notorious for yelling insults at his players, but they loved him. That's because they knew Lombardi loved them, even when he appeared to disrespect them.

Leadership style's not the issue. That's just perceived patterns of behavior, not necessarily a reflection of the internal capacity to love. In some style or personality types, it may take a little longer to determine if the capacity to love is present, but the lack of that capacity is almost always obvious.

Your employees will always be able to detect if you have a mean streak and a lack of love. But that doesn't mean you should fake caring about them because they'll also see through that, too. No matter how great your acting skills are, you can't pretend to love them without ever meaning it. Your actions speak louder than your words or body language. It's impossible to hide a lack of human caring and love. You actually have to possess sensitivity to your workers' needs. Do you even *see* what their needs are? Are you supplying what they need when they need it?

Granted, you do need some acting skills to get through horrendously bad days, no matter how loving you are. Acting encouraging and enthusiastic are much better options than ripping into your employees. You may feel like chopping them off at the knees, but show a little kindness when everyone's stressed out.

Be patient and kind.

The Pain of Working Without a Loving Boss

Most of us have worked for bosses who didn't love us or care about us. One boss I had years ago made me feel uncomfortable just to be in his presence. I was his chief financial officer (CFO) and very early on he made it clear he knew my job better than I did. He never really had to say anything to cause me to have self-doubts, but, after several months, I began to dread going to see him because of an unexplained fear. The situation kept getting worse and each encounter was a bad experience for me—probably for him as well.

I had a difficult time understanding what was happening until one day we were discussing another person who had caused some difficulties in the company.

"I don't trust him," said my boss. "But then, I don't trust anybody. And you, Gerry, your problem is you trust people. My advice to you is to recognize that the people who work for you are just human resources of business. You need to use them as if they were expendable. The only thing that matters is for us to get the job done. That means you need to check up on everything those people do."

His comments sent chills through me and I started looking for another position shortly after that conversation. Within six months, I was working for a different company.

That boss never understood how love and trust form the foundation of all human relationships. His employees didn't love or trust him because they knew he didn't express those attitudes toward them. Because of that, they felt no company loyalty and slacked off whenever he wasn't around. Since he couldn't check up on everybody all the time, and his subordinates didn't care whether he or the company was successful or not, their lack of loyalty ended up sabotaging his efforts. He failed as a leader and sank along with the company as it went into a tragic decline.

The employees failed because he failed.

Love Hurts

Loving others doesn't guarantee they'll love you. They may not reciprocate the caring you're showing them. The fact is some of your employees are probably lazy, dishonest, uncaring, unloving or just plain incompetent. But that still doesn't mean you shouldn't love them.

Remember, the love we're talking about is an action, not an emotion. It's what you do, not what you feel.

Sometimes you'll show your love for employees by being sensitive to their anxiety during difficult situations. At other times, you'll need to focus on their achievements and reinforce their successful actions.

It also means, at times, you'll have to discipline a serious misstep.

All of these actions are examples of love in action. They require more than just a faked, mechanical effort. Only when you love your associates can you perform these responsibilities with the sensitivity, compassion and firmness necessary to successfully achieve your organization's goals.

When parents show "tough love" to their children, it's usually because discipline is necessary to prevent them from harming themselves and those around them. If a teenager's caught driving drunk, the parents may take away his car keys to reinforce: a) it was a dangerous thing to do because the teen could have had a wreck and killed himself; b) he could have crashed into others and killed them; or c) the cycle of alcohol abuse unchecked has a potential to become a major adult problem, which will affect his jobs, marriage and other relationships.

The discipline is done with love because the parents love their sixteen-year-old child and want to protect him from inflicting further, perhaps more damaging, pain on himself and others. The parents have to be tough to get that teen back on the path to a better way of life, but just because they use discipline doesn't mean they don't love him. In fact, if they didn't love him, they wouldn't care what happened to him and would let him continue in his destructive behaviors, even to the point of death. (Unfortunately, there are parents like that.)

Leaders have to care about their employees, but, in order to reinforce required behavior, at times they'll have to show that love and caring through tough discipline.

Love isn't soft. It's tough enough to face reality.

Remember, the objective here is for your employees to achieve their goals and peak performance. You have to lead them to success by helping them incorporate behaviors which will get results. It's possible your positive, but firm, actions can turn around an employee's behavior. You never know until you try.

You're the most powerful force in their lives in the workplace. If you accept that heavy responsibility, then remember your love for them will be the best guide for your actions. It'll help you with the tough choices you have to make on a daily basis as their leader. You're wedged right in the middle between your organization's goals and your concern for your associates. There's no greater challenge than to maintain that balance.

Warren Bennis, author, advisor to four U.S. presidents and founding chairman of The Leadership Institute at the University of Southern California, wrote in his book *On Becoming a Leader*,

"Ultimately, a leader's ability to galvanize his or her co-workers resides both in self understanding and in understanding the co-workers' needs and wants..."[7]

To be a good leader, you have to go beyond understanding your own needs and wants. You have to understand what's motivating your employees, too.

Keep in mind few people want to fail. Failure's generally the result of well-intentioned people misdirecting their efforts. As a leader your responsibility is to help all your employees direct their efforts toward a successful result. The best way to accomplish that is to help them find the answers within themselves. When you assign them a task, you're showing them how to succeed at their jobs and when you help them discover their own potential, you're showing them how to succeed in life.

The only way you're going to accomplish that is if you have the capacity to love them and believe they have a right to the dignity which comes from personal achievement.

Self-Love Gives Us Strength and Confidence

As a leader, even before you focus on your employees, you have to love yourself. If you don't, you won't be able to love and care for anyone else.

Loving yourself in a healthy way will create a sense of peace within you. You know your strengths and weaknesses, your good qualities and your faults. You're in balance because you're able to accept yourself as you are. Self-love allows you to forgive yourself for your failings, while, at the same time, acknowledging your achievements.

"For self-renewing men and women the development of their own potentialities and the process of self-discovery never end," wrote the late statesman John William Gardner in his book *Self-Renewal.* "It is a sad but unarguable fact that most people go through their lives only partially aware of the full range of their abilities."[8]

Do you know the full range of your abilities?

Self-love isn't arrogance or conceit. It's accepting yourself as you are and being at peace with that. It means you recognize your own human frailties, but you aren't discouraged by what you see, all the while avoiding the pitfalls of self-pity, self-anger and other self-inflicted wounds. Instead, you keep moving forward, constantly improving yourself.

If you compare your knowledge, skills and capabilities to others, you probably are going to find someone who outshines you in one or all of those areas. But here's the thing: if you don't love yourself, you'll probably become angry because you're less capable than the individual you used as a benchmark comparison. That anger will, in turn, eat away at your own self-image and, in all likelihood, will be directed at the benchmark individual.

If you don't love yourself, when you perceive yourself falling short of others, you'll be unable to love them because of your own jealousy and self-loathing.

That's not productive for yourself or others.

How Do Your Employees See You?

Do your employees love you? If you were your own boss, would you love you?

To answer that, you're going to have to take a good, hard, honest, candid look at yourself in the mirror. What do you see?

Look back over the last week. How did you interact with your team members? Would you have wanted to have a boss react to you the way you reacted to your employees? Were you empathetic at the right time? Did you criticize them without constructive purpose? Did you listen to a complaint, then help your associate? Did you set an example in a time of crisis? Did you back off when you were wrong, or did you continue to try to prove you were right?

Do you like the boss you see in the mirror?

Have you ever been brave enough to ask your workers what they think of you? If you don't want to do it directly, there are organizations who can distribute employee surveys so you can gain a greater understanding of how you stand with your team. Sometimes, those kinds of surveys are the only effective way to get workers to tell you what they think.

However, they may tell you what you don't want to hear. Unfortunately, many bosses resist the results they get from employee feedback. Don't let self-absorption blind you to the truth your employees are giving you. Be humble enough to listen to what they have to say and make the changes which would be best for the team and the work environment. Don't look on it as a threat.

Instead, treat it as a learning opportunity. You'll be able to learn a great deal about yourself and how people perceive you.

If You Can't Love, Quit Trying to Be a Leader!

If you find you can't love and care for yourself or your employees, you should stop trying to be a Work Leader. If you'd rather do a job yourself than have the patience to help others succeed, quit your job as a leader. If you enjoy your own successful achievement of a task more than helping others succeed at the same task, then leave your current leadership position and get back to doing the task yourself.

If you try to lead without love, you'll fail.

If you'd rather do or say whatever you feel, then being a leader is the wrong role for you. You have to recognize the impact you have on your employees.

"Your own behavior has an impact around you," writes Dr. Beverly Potter in her book *Changing Performance on the Job*. "Things you do and say (or don't do and don't say) can function as antecedents that evoke—or as consequences that maintain—the behavior of someone else. The more you understand the interrelationships between your behaviors and the behaviors of subordinates, the more you can manage others by managing yourself."[9]

Only if you're capable of loving and caring about your employees will you be a good manager and boss. You should have greater joy seeing your workers succeed than in experiencing your own personal achievement. Do you enjoy helping others triumph over major obstacles? Do you love seeing your employees receive awards for success? Do you get satisfaction from seeing a previously unsuccessful worker achieve greatness?

As a leader, your satisfaction shouldn't be having accolades heaped on yourself, but rather in seeing someone else do a great job and succeed. If that describes you, you're the right person to be a Work Leader.

Keep reading and in the following chapters I'll show you how to channel your love for others into actions which will make you an even greater leader.

Case Study

Patricia had had a bad night and the morning was starting off even worse. She was not only late for work, but she dreaded her upcoming meeting with her boss at ten. She knew he was going to criticize her for being behind on her project. Her staff had failed her for months now, but she couldn't figure out what to do to get the project back on track.

Frank, her favorite project leader, had gotten far behind and she was always learning someone else in his group had decided to leave the company. Frank seemed to be trying everything, but was having no luck with his staff. Patricia was fed up with the entire project and with managing a bunch of incompetent and lazy people.

June, Patricia's least favorite manager, continued to annoy her. Every time she tried to get June to take on just a little more responsibility to help Frank get his project goals completed, June would respond with negative, complaining feedback.

"I'm already working sixty hours a week and I simply can't handle any more," June would tell her. "Why don't you figure out why Frank can't keep up?"

"How dare she try to tell me what I should do?" Patricia thought to herself. "She has no idea the challenges Frank has with his project. I'm sick of her whining. Maybe I ought to fire the entire lot, except for Frank, and start all over. Maybe with a new group of people, I could find at least a couple with the smarts and the drive to get quality work done."

Patricia also thought that was probably the best way to get her boss off her back. If she got rid of the people in her group, maybe her boss would give her a little more time. Firing everyone might make her look decisive and buy her at least three more weeks.

She left work feeling relieved with her decision, but when she got together with a group of friends from the company that night, they told her they were worried about her. They said they knew her boss was upset with her and she needed to get her project back on schedule.

Patricia didn't share her plan with them. She was convinced they'd all tell her she was being too tough, but there was no doubt in her mind she needed to get rid of the people she didn't like, particularly June, and rebuild her staff with those who would be loyal to her.

The next day, after she'd fired everyone but Frank and started the process of rehiring for those positions, Patricia felt great. She knew her new staff would soon bail out the project.

However, her boss didn't see it the same way. In fact, when she told him what she'd done, he was so angry, he fired her on the spot.

Questions

1. What could Patricia have done to save her job?

2. Patricia is capable of liking a subordinate, but is she capable of love?

3. Is Patricia's loyalty to Frank an admirable trait?

4. Was Frank a good performer? Did his performance warrant Patricia's loyalty?

5. What should Frank have done?

6. Why did Patricia ignore her friend's advice?

7. Why did Patricia fail to see she might lose her job because of the actions she took?

8. Would you like Patricia to be a friend of yours? If so, why? If not, why not?

9. What should Patricia do now?

10. Should Patricia be a manager?

chapter two

EXPECTATIONS
Set the Bar to Set the Tone

After understanding how love sets the tone for your relationship with your employees, your next step is to set expectations for your team. That's how you and your employees achieve success and it's where your real work of leadership begins.

Many will be familiar with the saying, "If you don't know where you're going, you'll wind up somewhere else." Without goals, you and your team have no direction. That's why you have to establish a clear vision for your workers, a mission with well-identified core values and goals, as well as a strategy to achieve those specific objectives. Give your employees a detailed action plan, laying out which tasks are needed to achieve peak performance.

If members of your team are saying things like, "How was I supposed to know what you wanted?" or, "Who do you think I am, a mind reader?" there's a good chance you aren't setting expectations and goals for them.

To be an effective leader, you have to be both a human relations specialist who meets your employees' needs, as well as a productivity specialist who meets your organization's needs, according to communications expert Dr. Thomas Gordon writing in his book *Leader Effectiveness Training*.[10]

That means you not only have to care for your workers, but you also have to guide them to their weekly and monthly goals, making sure they complete the jobs they've been assigned.

Your job as a Work Leader isn't to set your corporation's *overall* vision, strategy or goals. Your bosses will do that. But you do need to establish the objectives and agenda for your immediate work unit and those expectations have to match your company's goals.

That means don't waste time dreaming how the world could be better "if only." Focus on achieving the goals which will reward the entire organization with peak performance. Help your team focus on accomplishing tasks within a required time. Your job is to be mindful of the cost and make sure your employees are maintaining the quality which your bosses expect.

Realize you need to stay flexible and adjust to changing circumstances because expectations are fluid. The goals you set for this week may not be your company's goals next week. New technology or other changes in this fast-paced world may mean your unit will have to make a sudden left turn and stay flexible in order to adapt to the changes your organization needs.

When setting expectations, seven key components will help you achieve peak performance:

1. Keep it simple
2. Be specific
3. Measure results
4. Be prepared for resistance
5. Communicate team rules
6. Determine self-interest
7. Raise the bar

Let's take a look at each of these seven keys to success which will help you achieve your organization's goals.

1. Keep It Simple

The best way to communicate your action plan to your employees is to keep it as simple as possible.

Don't give your team members complicated and numerous instructions. That usually only leads to confusion. Instead, give them a few key goals so they have a clear understanding where they and the unit as a whole are moving.

Every great leader has achieved his or her success through simple strategies, plans and executions. Doing a few jobs better than anybody else is what makes McDonald's, Starbucks and Southwest Airlines so successful. True genius is having the ability to simplify the most complex situations and plans. The great scientist Albert Einstein came up with $E = mc^2$ to define the theory of relativity and with that, he changed the world of science. If a genius like Einstein can simplify his ideas to a few symbols, you can boil down your thoughts to a few key words, phrases or sentences.

Which of the following expectations is easier to understand?

1. We'll process all of our applications so they're perfect in every respect. That way customers will believe we're a caring, committed and focused company which has their best interests at heart, enabling them to trust us and get a product which satisfies their most critical expectations.

2. We'll provide customer satisfaction through processing applications with less than a .0001 percent error rate.

You'll probably agree the second option is simpler and, yet, far more powerful. It's specific and very focused on achieving peak performance.

Communicate your team's goals and expectations as simply as possible.

2. Be Specific

Your next step is to specifically define your organization's overall mission as it applies to your team members.

CEOs start with a very broad vision of what they want their company to achieve. They may say, "We want to put a PC in every home," or, "We want to delight our customers," or, "We want to be the largest company in the world." Their vision statement reflects what they want their company to do to reach "perfection." It's their highest ideal.

As a Work Leader, your mission statement to your team members breaks down those broader statements into more detailed plans. Whatever the level, each unit has to understand specifically what it's supposed to do. Sometimes your bosses will give you this information and other times you'll have to set the mission yourself.

The next step is for you to ask how you're going to accomplish your mission. What's your strategy and how specifically can you communicate that to your workers? You, as a Work Leader, need to put a magnifying glass up to your organization's big goals and see all the finer details necessary to actually bring about that plan. Only then can you begin to effectively set strategy and goals for your unit. Your expectation statement needs to be combined with a strategy for implementing it.

Work Leader's Tip: Establish Clear Expectations

- Does your organization have a vision statement? How about a mission statement? Do you think you need one? Have you made up your own? Does it match what your organization's written or have you gone off on your own journey?
- Do you have a clear understanding of the expectations your boss has for your work unit? Make a list of those expectations and explain what may be missing.
- When you set expectations for your staff, how did you decide who got what goals? Did they participate in the goal setting? Should they have been involved?
- When your boss last told you how you were doing, what did he say? Were his expectations being met? If not, why not? If yes, then how did that happen? Did you do the work yourself? Did your staff do it? What's your secret for success in meeting your boss's expectations?
- There are times when we have the ability to do more than is expected of us. Is there anything you think your organization needs which you could be providing? Have you talked to your boss about taking on that responsibility?
- Is there any chance your boss already thinks you're doing something to achieve that result? Could he have hidden expectations of you which you haven't been assigned in your formal goal-setting process with your boss?
- What's the relationship of the expectations you have for your staff to those your boss has for you? If your staff meets your expectations, will you impress your boss? If not, why not? Is there anything you can do to make your expectations of your staff more closely linked to what your boss expects of your unit?

Let's look at a few examples.

If your CEO says, "Our company's going to manufacture parts for the aviation industry," you might then turn around to your team and tell them their mission is to make the final stamping operation for airframe components, with a strategy of using modern flow manufacturing techniques to minimize inventory requirements and reduce rework.

If you're an accounting supervisor and your CEO says, "We're going to provide accounting services to small business entrepreneurs," you'd tell your workers their mission is to manage the bank reconciliation efforts for all your clients. You could then give them a strategy of utilizing a marketing concept of selling only to franchises of major chains, while developing a system to have automated reconciliation on all accounts over a given size.

If you're a proposal section manager and your CEO says, "As a charitable foundation, we're going to fund a select group of organizations," you'd tell your employees their mission is to evaluate proposals of your existing client organizations to find seed funding for new projects which support battered or abused women. You could then tell them your strategy is to solicit funds from people who have just sold dramatically appreciated stock and are looking for maximize tax advantages, while finding ways to identify key factors impacting your prospects' decisions.

3. Measure Results

Once your bosses have determined your organization's overall direction, you, as a Work Leader, need to find tangible ways to measure your team's progress toward the goals. Get very detailed. Setting very specific, detailed and measurable goals and objectives is the essence of successful leadership.

Ambiguous expectations create ambiguous results. If expectations aren't measurable, everybody can claim an objective has been met— no matter what the result. If your staff thinks the results may be disputed, then you can be certain they will be. You have to find some way to be able to evaluate the performance against the expectations. Make sure measurement is easy and obvious.

For instance, if you're a sales manager, set a goal that each member of your team will call on thirty prospects a month in order to sign up at least two new customers. In addition, those new customers need to order at least $100,000 in new parts, which have to be delivered within three weeks of the order date.

If you're a section supervisor in a manufacturing plant, your goal might be to produce 500 airfoils per day, with a .005 percent or less rework rate, at a cost of less than $35 per unit and with 99.9 percent delivered by a specific date.

If you're an office manager, your goal might be to have all current documents filed by the end of each work day.

Work Leader's Tip: What an Expectation Looks Like

Anything your staff routinely does to achieve the goals of your enterprise is a potential area for expectation setting. Don't set expectations for tasks which will not contribute directly to the success of your unit.

Below are some examples of tasks where you should establish expectations:

- Number of tax returns completed each day
- Customers serviced per day
- Errors made per hour
- Applications processed per day
- Parts produced per hour
- Lawns cut per day
- Incoming phone calls handled per hour
- Sales made per month
- Cars repaired per day
- Lines of code written per hour
- Haircuts completed per hour
- Accounts reconciled per hour
- Parts produced per hour
- Complaints handled per hour
- Prescriptions filled per day
- Orders processed per hour
- Applications processed per hour
- Complaints resolved per hour

Your goal is to eliminate ambiguity. Set goals, objectives and action plans which can be measured quantitatively and make sure you decide in advance how you're going to *easily* and *efficiently* measure the performance. If you decide to measure an expectation a certain way, then discover later that measurement process is too time-consuming, costly or inaccurate, you've created a problem in evaluating your team's progress.

The only exception to this, and a reason not to measure, is if your goal is more qualitative and academic than quantitative.

As a Work Leader you need to know what your bosses expect of you, just as your employees need to know what you expect of them. If your workers don't know your expectations, they'll end up setting their own, which could put your unit far afield from the goals of your organization. And, when the time comes to evaluate their performance, you won't have a standard to apply. You can't have your workers guess at what's expected of them. It's your duty as a leader to make sure your goals and, ultimately, their goals coincide with those of your organization.

4. Be Prepared for Resistance

Any idea you take to your staff will almost always be met with resistance. True, your success will be largely dependent on how well you get your employees' support, but don't waste time trying to get everyone on board. You need to be prepared to settle for less than 100 percent buy-in to your direction. Just accept the fact that no matter what you say or how persuasive you and others may be in presenting new ideas and expectations, not every member of your staff is going to agree with every facet of the operation.

Don't let that statement discourage you. Even the naysayers may buy in to some of your plan. Consider that a victory.

Your employees will be at one of three levels: **understanding**, **acceptance** or **agreement**.

If they **understand** your direction and expectations, what they're expected to do and what it'll take to achieve results which meet the goals, even if they don't agree, they'll still move forward toward your goal, just not as enthusiastically, and they may fight you on certain aspects of it.

If they understand and **accept** your expectations for success and you and your organization's right to establish the direction, they may not totally agree, but they won't fight you and will work to meet your expectations.

If they understand, accept and **agree** with you, they'll believe you're guiding the team in the correct direction with the proper measurement of their performance. They're all in.

The ideal level of buy-in is agreement, but if you only get acceptance, take it and move on. What you've gotten is recognition your expectation works, even though they personally wouldn't have chosen it.

Work Leader's Tip: **Set Specific Expectations**

Here are a few examples of making your goals specific, measurable and effective:

- **Tax returns prepared.**
  Each accountant will complete an average of ten tax returns per day during the tax season.
- **Customers serviced.**
  During each quarter, each branch customer service representative will process to completion an average of twenty-five walk-in customers per day with an average score of "highly satisfied" on the customer satisfaction survey.
- **Errors made.**
  Each machine in the production unit will produce at an average reject rate of not greater than .005 percent.
- **Sales calls made.**
  Each salesperson will make a minimum of 250 calls to prospects from the corporate office's lead list.
- **Haircuts completed.**
  Each stylist will, each week, complete an average of 2.7 cuts per hour, with a redo rate of not greater than .5 percent.
- **Orders processed.**
  Each processor will ship a minimum of 99 percent of all orders received in a day.

In the long run, if the expectation is fair, staff members will probably begin to agree. Save your powers of persuasion for another day and another issue.

5. Communicate Team Rules

As a leader, you must communicate another type of expectation to your associates: what you expect of them as members of the organization.

You must make certain each person in your organization knows what the rules are for being part of the team. These rules could be as simple as being at at work on time every day or as complex as expecting each person to hit a specific quality standard for output, a certain volume standard for productivity and a certain cleanliness standard at each work station.

It's essential that all team members remember a team works together and an individual must bend to the benefit of the team.

"Teamwork is the fabric of effective business organizations," writes Norman Augustine in his book *Augustine's Laws*. The aerospace businessman and former Under Secretary of the U.S. Army stresses how important unity is to a team. "Soloists are inspiring in opera and perhaps even in small entrepreneurial ventures, but there is no place for them in large corporations. This is most assuredly not to say there is no place for the individualist, only that it is necessary for members of the team to be willing to suppress individual desires for the overall good of the team."[11]

But in order to work together as a team, your employees need to know how you expect them to do that. Your team's rules should state clearly what expectations you have about integrity, courtesy, team participation, safety and a host of other traits which set the tone for everyday activity. That includes how you're going to deal with conflict, what you expect from group discussions and how you expect them to share feedback with each other.

Clearly communicate your team's rules to each employee in your unit.

6. Determine Self Interest

It's a safe bet your employees probably aren't trying to get you a promotion, especially if they think you're a great leader. If that's the case, they'd probably prefer you stay right where you are. Nobody wants

| Work Leader's **Tip:** | **Practice Understanding, Acceptance and Agreement** |

Make certain your associates know what's expected of them and what they need to do to achieve success. Agreement and having 100 percent buy-in to your direction is only possible when you've made your goals crystal clear. Remember, understanding is an essential first step to acceptance. Ask yourself these questions to be certain your employees understand:

- Pick one subordinate who's been achieving the least and identify the expectations you have for that person. Does he or she know precisely what you expect? If not, did you make the goals clear? Are they written down?
- Pick the best subordinate you have and write down the expectations he or she has most effectively achieved. How do you know the performance is effective? What's the measurement you used? Does that associate really understand? If so, what did you do differently than with the one who doesn't understand?
- You probably have some personal tasks which contribute to the results of the unit. How much of the performance of your work unit is completely tied to your personal performance? Is there an associate who should be doing the job, but isn't because he or she doesn't understand or accept your assignment? Have you explained the need to accept that assignment?
- Do you have such a secret wish for certain employees, such as, "If only Joe could do that"? What's kept you from expecting Joe to accomplish that goal? What can you do to get that task assigned to Joe? Does Joe understand his assignment?
- Do all members of your work unit have a clear set of expectations? Do they understand and accept them or have you failed to effectively communicate them? Make a list of each person who may not know what the expectations are for his or her job and create a list of individual expectations for them. Once you've completed that list, what do you plan to do with it?

to lose a great boss.

On the other hand, if they don't like you, they still don't want you to get a promotion. They want you fired.

Employees, like most people, are pretty self-centered. It's not that they're uncaring. It's more that they're thinking about their own lives, problems and issues. They're looking forward to their futures—and they want a promotion for themselves. Even if you're the best boss they ever had, your success isn't likely to be their highest priority.

Whatever expectations you have for your workers, they're not trying to achieve those goals to make you look good or have the company beat the competition. They're trying to achieve organizational peak performance expectations or goals for their own personal advancement. They're much more likely to be interested in what success is going to come their way.

Remember that when you set expectations for them. Make sure they know what achieving company goals means to them personally. Then their success will translate into your organization's success, as well as your own.

Imagine what your staff members are thinking. If they meet your expectation, does that mean they're going to be forced to work ten hours of overtime a week? If so, that's going to cut into their personal time with their families and friends. Why should they make that sacrifice for you and the company? If they can't see how it directly benefits them, they're not going to be too motivated. If they work the overtime, will they get time-and-a-half or double pay for those hours? Will they get a promotion? Or will their only reward be exhaustion and the threat of being fired if they don't?

"What's in it for me?" is a natural question and as a Work Leader, you have to be able to answer it.

Find ways to use your employees' self-interests to the advantage of your organization. When individuals' efforts satisfy their own self-interests, they'll increase productivity—something which will benefit the person, the team and the entire organization.

7. Raise the Bar

Setting expectations higher than previous performance levels is an essential part of achieving peak performance. Work Leaders must constantly be looking for opportunities to "raise the bar." That's because complacent organizations which are satisfied with the status quo rarely reach the highest level of success. You can't hold on to existing success, hoping it will continue without any additional effort. You have to constantly be searching for new ways to exceed that and stretch for new growth.

Always strive to increase your own personal achievement, as well as that of your team. You can't set an example which is weak or easy. It's only when you as a leader raise the bar on achieving goals that your employees will also. They follow your lead.

"No team ever finishes ahead of its leader," wrote management guru Joe D. Batten in his book *Tough-Minded Leadership*. "A true responsive leader must dare to stand out from the crowd."[12]

Focus on challenging your employees to stretch their abilities and talents to that next level, something slightly higher than they've stretched before. It doesn't have to be a huge stretch. Go in increments. When you and your team achieve success with one small step it'll encourage all of you to try for even higher goals.

However, avoid pushing your employees too hard to reach higher. That can create frustration in your team when employees aren't ready to jump hurtles that high. Take them slowly to higher levels. Balance is crucial.

How *Not* to Raise the Bar

The following exchange between a Work Leader and an employee illustrates the pain which results from trying to raise the bar too much too quickly. Once you go too far, the resistance can get so severe, almost anything you say can result in your employees refusing to try because of frustration. If you ask for too much, you may get nothing.

> WORK LEADER: I've set a new goal of increasing our processing from ten files a day to twenty-five.
> ASSOCIATE: We've been doing ten a day for the last five years. How is that increase even possible?
> WORK LEADER: We have a new process we believe will help increase productivity.
> ASSOCIATE: Then why change it now before we know about the process?

WORK LEADER: I want to provide you with a new challenge so we can take advantage of the gains.

ASSOCIATE: Why should I increase output by that much?

WORK LEADER: Because the company needs to increase its productivity.

ASSOCIATE: Why do I care about that?

WORK LEADER: Company profits will make us all better off.

ASSOCIATE: How?

WORK LEADER: We'll make more money and there'll be more money in profit sharing.

ASSOCIATE: I'm not eligible for profit sharing.

WORK LEADER: You will be.

ASSOCIATE: Yes, but I'm not now. What's in it for me today?

WORK LEADER: You get a chance to hit a new goal and have the fun of being better.

ASSOCIATE: Are you cutting staff and just trying to get me to pick up the slack?

WORK LEADER: No, but we'll be able to take on more work with the same staff.

ASSOCIATE: What if we don't get any more work? Are you going to cut staff then?

WORK LEADER: We're confident we'll be able to get greater volumes of work.

ASSOCIATE: Are you going to pay me more?

WORK LEADER: No, not right now. Meet the new expectations and you'll be more eligible for promotion.

ASSOCIATE: What kind of promotion?

WORK LEADER: I don't have a specific one in mind right now.

ASSOCIATE: Are you going to pay me more money?

WORK LEADER: Not right now. Maybe later, if you meet new expectations.

ASSOCIATE: Maybe? Are you kidding?

The task of setting expectations too high can be risky. Goals are designed to bring about a new course, but a new direction seldom comes easily.

As the sixteenth century Italian diplomat and historian Niccolo

Machiavelli wrote in his political treatise *The Prince,* "It must be considered that there is nothing more difficult to carry out, nor more doubtful of success, nor more dangerous to handle, than to initiate a new order of things."[13]

New, higher goals for your team are doable only if you make them something your employees can manage. Set the bar to impossibly steep heights and you'll have an unhappy and unproductive group of employees on your hands.

People enjoy being challenged as long as what they're reaching for is something they can actually accomplish. Make the goal impossible and you face failure for them and yourself.

Case Study

"Kim, I'm very concerned about our division's sales," said Carol. "We've been falling behind and I think your performance is having a serious impact on the team as a whole. What are you going to do to pick up the pace?"

Kim sat in complete silence for thirty seconds. Finally she said, "I don't understand. I've been on my personal plan for the entire year. How can you suggest I'm the one failing? I'm probably the only one who's going to exceed my previous year's actual sales."

Carol was stunned. Kim's sales were good, but her ten-percent increase simply wasn't going to be enough. "You know the plan for this year calls for a twenty-percent increase."

"I told you last December I couldn't do twenty percent," said Kim. "In fact, I thought the best I could do was five percent, but I committed to ten percent because I wanted to show you I'd really push myself. I never committed to anything like twenty percent."

"I know you wanted the goal to be ten percent," said Carol, "but top management said it needed to be twenty percent and that's what I com-mitted to. I can't have a shortfall."

"How can you tell me halfway through the year my goal is a twenty-percent increase? You never told me that. I'm very confused and, frankly, angry. I can't get twenty percent. You should have known that and told top management. Also, I happen to know no other salesperson in the division has a goal of anything close to twenty percent."

Questions

1. Why did Kim fail when she felt she was succeeding?

2. What should Carol have done to make certain Kim was a success?

3. Could Kim succeed on her own?

4. If Carol had made certain Kim had a clear understanding of her expectations, would Carol have been responsible for Kim's failure?

5. Kim is a "successful failure." Whose fault is that?

6. If you were Kim's boss, what would you have done differently?

7. Have you ever been in the situation where Kim finds herself? What did you do?

8. Have you ever made the same mistake Carol made? If so, what would you do now?

chapter three

ASSIGNMENT
Square Pegs Never Fit Round Holes

After setting expectations to lay the groundwork for leading an organization, you need employees who are going to meet those expectations. Finding the best staff is essential.

To find people who have the values, abilities, performance and attitudes you need to win the competitive race to excellence, you can't compromise on the quality of your hires. The last thing you need is to end up with a staff made up of people who don't have the proper qualities for success.

But it's not just finding the right people. It's making sure your new hires are a good fit with your company and your immediate team. More than "matching" the qualifications for a vacant position, you need to make sure new hires fit your company. It's especially important to remember square pegs don't fit round holes.

Absolutely the first consideration is hiring the very best people you can find. Nothing's more disastrous to an organization than having members of your staff who don't measure up. Hire only those who are as good as, or better than, your current employees.

That means don't rush the process. Take time to find excellent people and don't try to fill your job vacancies too quickly. If you do, there's a good chance you'll end up with employees who aren't well suited to your organization or your individual team.

Hiring a person who not only lacks quality education, skills and personality traits, but also isn't a good fit with your organization, can be more of a problem than you not filling the position at all. The wrong hire has the potential to soak up your time with problems and chaos they'll leave behind them. Take your time finding the best candidates, even before you lock in the specific direction you're going.

That's because many companies may find they need to suddenly change direction to survive. You want to make sure you hire those who not only fit with employees in your particular area, but also fit with the company as a whole—even when it needs to pursue new options. If you hire someone merely because they match the direction your organization's currently going, he or she may not be able to adapt to the changes you and your organization make a few months or years down the line.

Having the vision to see if a potential hire will fit with your team is the mark of a great leader.

"Great vision without great people is irrelevant," writes business consultant and author James C. Collins in his book *Good to Great: Why Some Companies Make the Leap... and Others Don't.* He says if you successfully hire the right employees, "the problem of how to motivate and manage people largely goes away. The right people don't need to be tightly managed or fired up; they will be self-motivated by the inner drive to produce the best results and to be part of creating something great."[14]

Collins adds, "The executives who ignited the transformations from good to great did not first figure out where to drive the bus and then get people to take it there. No, they first got the right people on the bus (and the wrong people off the bus) and then figured out where to drive it...It all starts with disciplined people. The transition begins not by trying to discipline the wrong people into the right behaviors, but by getting self-disciplined people on the bus in the first place."

Find the best people, then place them in the proper positions for their skills and steer them in the direction you need them to go. The vision comes after your hire them.

First Understand the Process

Now that you've hired the best people, how do you decide what their specific assignment of duties will be? Unfortunately, many leaders don't focus on the assignment part of the process.

First, you have to decide what the job or position really is and how it fits into the work process of your organization. This "systems approach" to evaluating all the jobs in your group is essential if you're going to help people achieve the goals of your company. True, the end result is essential, but, all too often, bad managers forget it's the process which determines success.

If you tell your employees, "I don't care how you do it, just get the backlog out by tomorrow," but you don't mention what kind of quality you're expecting, your workers may cut corners and ignore the impact on your unit's other responsibilities, especially to other sections in the company.

How employees get the job done *does* matter. If a process is designed to make each sequential element achieve specific results, then the entire process will be more likely to achieve superior results. It does matter what the elements are in the system. Leaders have to know those elements and continue to improve on their achievement. In order to assign a task, leaders first have to know if the task really is necessary, why it's necessary and what defines effective completion.

Most importantly, your employees need to know why accomplishing their tasks is essential to the mission of the organization.

There are a lot of reasons you may try to skip the assignment part of the process. It could be your boss instructed you not to change anything or mess with the established way your organization runs things. Or it could be because you yourself are either overworked or a bit lazy and you're avoiding that step because the process is hard work or takes too long.

Whatever the reason, you have to develop a clear knowledge, not just of the process and the jobs within it, but how your employees' work or their lack of quality affects others in the organization. What one associate does not only has an influence on the other workers in your immediate unit, but also on other units in your company. Your entire organization is working toward the goal of providing a finished product or service to either external or internal customers. Whatever happens in your unit, ultimately, affects your company's customers one way or another.

If the process you manage isn't functioning properly, if it doesn't produce the intended result effectively, then you have to fix it. A broken process not only can destroy an organization, but it can also destroy the individual assigned to it.

Before you make an assignment, think about whether your

company's process is making success impossible for members of your unit. If so, fix that first, in whatever way is possible. To do that, you may need to get creative in order to skirt the inertia in your company which frowns on any changes. Make these decisions with love, but remember: to ensure your team's success, you need to fix what's broken first.

Look at the Job Description
Why create a job description? You may be thinking, "My staff knows what to do. Why waste time writing a description?"

Work Leader's Tip: **How To Find The Best Employees**

One of the great challenges in assigning great people is finding them. You can't pick great hires if you don't have great candidates.

Here are some ideas which should help:

- Make friends with your in-house recruiter.
- Talk to your staff. The best prospects can come from friends of your best employees.
- Look for people you encounter in retail shops who give you good service.
- Talk to your friends about people they know.
- Ask people in your family about their friends, but don't hire family members.
- Talk to acquaintances from your church, synagogue or mosque. Their values may be similar to yours.
- Ask people you know from service clubs like Rotary and Lions Club.
- Join the chamber of commerce in your local area and go to the networking meetings.
- If you get an interesting résúme, interview the person even if you have no opening.
- Look at everybody you meet as a potential associate. In short, you should always be recruiting.

That's a classic argument. It does take discipline to organize your department's job requirements and some leaders, unfortunately, don't want to take the time to do that step. But the fact still remains that every staff member needs to know what to do. Your employees need that structure before they can move forward. That's why you need a formal job description. Imagine what would happen if certain service professionals didn't know what their specific jobs were.

"Firemen cannot stop each time they arrive at a new fire to figure out who will attach the hose to the hydrant and who will go up the ladder," writes Canadian author and business management professor Henry Mintzberg in his book *Structure in Fives: Designing Effective Organizations.* "Similarly, airline pilots must be very sure about their landing procedures well in advance of descent."[15]

Imagine the chaos and inefficiency of time which would, in most cases, result in a loss of life if firefighters and pilots didn't know what they were supposed to do and when.

Before your employees begin working, you, as their Work Leader, need to know and understand each aspect of their jobs.

Begin by asking yourself these questions:

- What does each person need to do?
- Is the work manual, where your employees are mainly using their hands, or is the work a job which requires their mental abilities to think through a complex problem?
- What are the working hours?
- When do you need the end product or service?
- How much will your organization allow you to pay for the right person?
- Where does the person need to work: at home or in the office?
- Do your employees need specific knowledge or skills?
- Do they need to have that knowledge or skills prior to being hired or is it better if you train them?

That's just a basic list. Granted, it's easier if your organization's already written a position description, but even if that's the case, you'll still need to ask many critical questions about each job. Even if you don't have previous knowledge or experience with the jobs you need to assign, you still have to evaluate the positions and assign specific duties and performance requirements.

And it's not a one-time thing. You're going to have to keep writing and tweaking your descriptions. Most probably aren't totally accurate when they're newly written and they'll definitely become dated and obsolete pretty quickly—possibly even before the month is over.

If you're blessed with a great employee who performs well, you can be sure he or she not only is doing what the job description says, but is going beyond that, performing tasks not specified or even modifying the method of achieving the end result because it's more efficient and leads to better quality. Take note of that for the next time you need to write a description and incorporate your star performer's adaptations to the job requirements.

If an employee consistently overperformed and took on additional tasks, but you don't put that into the description and the new hire only does what you've stated is required, you're going to be disappointed. You've become accustomed to your former high performers because they went a step above the requirements. It's not your new hire's fault. The newcomer didn't know that.

New associates may need to speak to their predecessors to find out all aspects of the position when they held it. If that's not possible, maybe you and your new hires need to go back to the process and find out how their jobs fit into the "bigger picture." It's your duty to resolve the confusion long before the new associate arrives. If you can't do that, then at least you'll need to give the newcomer some time and understanding until you both can redefine the job.

Writing a Useful Job Description

Almost every organization has a job description system, but new jobs may not have been formally documented. If your bosses haven't given you a description for a job which falls within your authority, it may work in your favor and give you the opportunity to come up with your own version.

Here are some simple steps you can follow to make sure you and your candidates have a clear understanding of what the job is:

A. Define Expectations

First, start by defining the results required of the job. This takes us back to the expectations we talked about in the previous chapter. You have to carefully define what success on the job really means for the associate and the organization. If the job is to process applications for a loan, then define what a "processed loan" means. What should it look like? How will you know it's done well? What's the expected quality of the paperwork? How many loans should be accomplished in a day? In short, define the outputs of the job.

B. Process

After you've done the expectations, you have to specify how the job gets done. It may be the way it was done before you had the opening, or a completely new way to approach things. Do this in a detailed manner so you can use it as a training document for the new individual as well. If you know how to draw a flow chart, make one. If you're more comfortable with a step-by-step list of the actions required, do that. Since few jobs have only one task the person has to do, you'll need to make a list for each element of the job. Make certain it defines clearly what the person will be doing each and every day.

C. Requirements

Define what it takes to be able to do this job. Here you should write down the knowledge, skills and attitudes the applicant has to have in order to be successful. If the person needs to be good at numbers and skilled in operating a calculator, make that clear. If the associate needs no previous knowledge of processing loans, make that clear as well. In every respect, be very specific about the core requirements any candidate has to have in order to be successful.

The Requirements of the Job Versus the Abilities of the Person

Knowing what has to be done is only the first step. Knowing what it takes to do a job is the second.

The whole process of assigning people to tasks really turns on your ability to pick people with the ability to succeed—those who have the knowledge, skills, and attitudes to do the tasks involved.

Realize that those hires not possessing those qualities will fail.

Employees may be able to refine their knowledge and skills on the job, but if they come with significant shortages, you may find yourself waiting a long time for them to meet your expectations. In fact, they'll probably fail first.

"All too many people have been placed in positions that, on the one hand, make relatively little use of their real aptitudes and interests and, on the other hand, make demands upon them in areas where they are the weakest," writes Richard A. Fear in his book *The Evaluation Interview: Predicting Job Performance in Business and Industry.*[16]

The same is true about attitudes. It's not that you can't change attitudes, but the journey from weak and negative attitudes to good, strong and positive attitudes is painful, stressful and uncertain.

Don't waste your time being a social worker when it comes to attitude. If a candidate reflects a negative attitude, move on. Life as a leader is already a challenge. Don't add to it by trying to be a psychotherapist. We'll focus more on this when we discuss development and evaluation.

Determining Characteristics

How do you determine what key characteristics a successful candidate should have?

First, start with the functions of the job.

If the position calls for somebody to talk to customers and ask them for personal information, it's essential for the candidate to have good communications skills, a capacity for sincerity and a sensitivity to people's anxieties. If a candidate lacks interpersonal skills or seems introverted, you need to consider another person for the role.

If the role requires strong financial analysis skills, a person with no accounting background and without a strong systematic thought process would probably be a failure.

Job assignment is the process of matching job requirements with personal abilities. A mismatch is almost always a prescription for disaster. Some shortcomings may be corrected remedially, but, if the core capabilities for accomplishing the job tasks are missing, both you and the candidate will be unsuccessful and unhappy. Don't set up candidates for failure just because you think they're good people.

Although positive attitudes are essential, they're not sufficient.

Good attitudes can make up for many weaknesses, but they can't make up for a lack of capabilities.

Skills and core personal competencies matter, but personal characteristics vary greatly. Some can be critical to success and will be obvious. Others may not.

Work Leader's Tip: **How Do You Look For The Right Qualities In A Candidate?**

There is no foolproof way to make the right hiring decision. The key is to focus on what really matters, not on questions which are easy to answer.

Don't ask questions which:

- Can be answered by reading a résúme or by doing reference checks
- Are illegal by virtue of federal or state statute
- Pose political, philosophical or religious issues
- Are personal and have nothing to do with how candidate will do in the work environment
- Have nothing to do with the candidate's ability or interest in doing the job

Do ask questions which:

- Help you understand what the person has really done in previous jobs, such as, "What were your duties?"
- Ask the applicant about actions taken under specific circumstances, such as, "What did you do when...?"
- Reveal accomplishments and how they were measured, such as, "What were the results of...?"
- Cause the person to show problem-solving skills, such as, "How would you handle...?"
- Prove the candidate's general interests and goals, such as, "What is your career goal in five years?"
- Probe the candidate's self-awareness, such as, "What are the things you do best? What don't you do well?"

Some examples of what to look for might be:

- An attention to detail and basic arithmetic skills for accounting clerk candidates
- Steady hands for machinist candidates
- Strong verbal skills and the ability to deal with a broad range of hard-selling vendor personnel for purchasing clerk candidates
- Someone who can patiently receive insults from irate customers for a customer service representative position
- Basic arithmetic and a pleasant demeanor under stress for bank teller candidates
- Logical, structured thinking skills for systems analyst candidates

These things may seem obvious to you, but, unfortunately, not all managers take these things into consideration and end up with problems later. It's essential you know and understand how these types of personal characteristics might impact success in any given job.

Make sure candidates have the right skills and the right attitudes and you'll have a much better chance of achieving peak performance.

Strong Résumes and Weak Interviews

You absolutely shouldn't interview a candidate whose résume fails to pass the key criteria for education, experience and the results which a position requires.

Be determined to find a candidate who has the majority of characteristics you consider necessary for the job. Those words on a résume aren't the true measure of someone's knowledge and skills, but they're still a critical first step in evaluating the person.

A candidate is seldom going to look better than what you see on a carefully crafted résume. If you compromise at this point, you'll be lowering the bar you've established for the initial filtering process. Keep your expectations high. Don't waste your time on candidates who simply don't meet the minimum requirements of the job. Even in the tightest of labor markets, capable people are available and you need to use your time to recruit them.

One useful technique is to carefully review candidate résumes during the initial sorting process. Pick those having the apparent best qualifications, make a short list of candidates to interview, then put the résumés aside. When the time for a candidate interview comes, avoid rereading the résumé prior to the interview and concentrate your energy on the interview. This focuses your attention on interviewing the person, not the résumé.

Unfortunately, some candidates lie about their education, experience or skills on their résumés. Because of that, take part of your interview to explore more fully the areas you didn't fully understand, as well as areas you think might have been misstatements or misperceptions.

Because of a résumé's brevity, providing the bare-bones of their work career, you may not understand all a person has really accomplished in his or her career. That piece of paper only tells you what a candidate did and lists a few key successes, but it won't give you key insights into the person's knowledge, skills, attitudes and behaviors.

Let's say a candidate worked as an accounts payable clerk for five years. You really need to find out what he did, how his success was measured and how he achieved success. It's essential you understand how those criteria fit your expectations of the job you're trying to fill.

If you're hiring a hair stylist, you'll need to find out how her previous customers viewed her performance. How did the stylist generate new customers? What was her productivity?

If you're hiring a lawyer, what's the best way to determine the person's research capability? How can you know what her client satisfaction was? Is the attorney capable of sound analysis?

Prior behavior is a great predictor of future behavior, so don't let yourself think a person will change. What you're looking for are behaviors which will help individuals be successful at your organization. You're also looking for someone who has demonstrated success and who will match your expectations of the knowledge, skills and attitudes you require. You're not doing social work. You want winners, so look for them and hire them.

A résumé is a candidate's statement of what he or she thinks you want to know or should know. Sometimes that effort's successful, but many times it's not. Your goal as an interviewer is to determine whether the person has the ability to fill your needs.

Short of mind reading, you won't be able to know if a candidate fits your organization unless you spend time probing his or her history of accomplishments, learning and growth potential. That's why the interview really is the most valuable assignment tool you have at your disposal.

That applies to internal candidates, as well as those you're hiring

---

Work Leader's Tip: Control Everything About The Interview

Most Work Leaders try hard to not appear as a "controlling personality," but in an interview, you need to have that trait. Don't allow an applicant to control the interview. This is your time to make a judgment about the person and you need to be on your agenda, not his. Do it with courtesy, but make sure you're in charge.

Here are some tips to controlling the interview:

- Have the interview location set up well in advance. Be organized.
- Take applicants to the location and direct their movement. You lead the way.
- Have the environment match your leadership style, whether it's informal or formal.
- Tell applicants you'll be asking a number of questions first. Their questions come at the end.
- Prepare a list of questions you're going to ask and make sure you ask them.
- Always get an answer to your questions.
- Bore deeply to get to the details.
- Focus on listening to the answers. Never let a question go by without a follow-up question.
- Probe behaviors and work experiences. Ask what they did, not how they felt.
- If you pose hypothetical questions, let them have time to think, but not too long.
- Tie your questions to their résúme. Get examples of what they did, how it worked and why.

from outside the company. You always have to do a legitimate and thorough interview of all candidates, even those you work with every day. Familiarity is no reason to forgo your opportunity to interview candidates.

A résúme is a wealth of information, but the interview will be the key to your discovery.

"The purpose of an interview is to: select a good performer, educate him as to who you and the company are, determine if a mutual match exists, and sell him on the job," wrote engineer and former CEO of Intel Corporation Andrew S. Grove in his book *High Output Management.*[17]

Close Your Mouth and Open Your Mind

The most serious mistake you can make in the interview process is to do all the talking. The best interviews are those where your candidate speaks at least ninety-five percent of the time and you actively listen. If you're doing all the talking, it's going to be difficult for you to listen as carefully as you need to in order to gather all the necessary information.

Obviously, your questions are crucial, but your candidate's answers are even more important. You already know about yourself. Your goal has to be to learn about the candidate. If you're listening carefully, you can branch off from his or her answers to craft more questions which will probe a bit further into experiences. Never underestimate the value of follow-up questions.

Close your mouth, open your ears, engage your brain, then ask a question. Listen to the response, process the answer, then ask follow-up questions. That's the sequence of activity required for active listening. If you do anything else, you're interviewing yourself.

Don't accept a candidate's "sound bite." You have to focus on the details of the answer by getting both a broad and a deep understanding of how the candidate succeeded in previous work environments.

Don't ask questions which the candidate can easily answer with "yes" or "no" responses. If you ask open-ended questions, you'll gather more information. Ask questions like, "Give me an example of how you managed your worst customer problem." Or, "Tell me about the time you spent at Mega Corporation as a financial analyst." Or, "Tell me about your first job and how you liked your first boss."

Vague questions will get vague answers. Never ask a question which allows a candidate to give a theoretical or conceptual answer unless you're looking for critical thinking skills. Questions like, "What is a good employee?" may be good at getting an intellectual insight into employee management, but it won't give you specific insights into a candidate's behavior.

Instead, you might try, "How did you handle the problem when you had a fellow associate who wasn't getting the job done effectively and was getting you and your unit into difficulty with management?"

What you want are answers to what candidates have actually done and how they achieved results. Remember, you're looking for winners. The only way to find them is to probe for their successes and how they achieved them.

In chapter one, we described the differences between love and like. This message carries over throughout this book and it has direct application in your hiring interviews. You can't afford to like a candidate. You have to always be on guard against strongly liking a résúme before you've had the opportunity to interview a candidate. Enter an interview with an open mind.

Just as importantly, you have to not allow yourself to be influenced by liking a candidate during your interview. This is even harder. We've all had the experience of feeling a "chemistry" and connection with someone within seconds of meeting them, but remember you're hiring the whole person. Liking a candidate can severely constrain the objectivity you need to determine if that person will fit your specific job, your team or your corporation. Certainly, if the chemistry is bad, it may portend a relationship problem in the future, but good chemistry isn't a predictor of high-quality job performance. In fact, strong positive chemistry frequently has an adverse impact on a leader's ability to effectively manage an associate. You probably should avoid hiring people you don't like, but don't simply hire all candidates you like.

Hire those you love because they're highly qualified. Hire those who, through past experiences, have demonstrated they have the knowledge, skills, attitudes and behaviors they need to help you achieve great results for the organization. Any other reasons should fall way down the list of selection criteria.

Hiring from Within

When a vacancy comes up in your organization, the natural tendency is to fill the job from within. That has all the obvious benefits of offering growth opportunities to existing staff, while at the same time allowing you to deal with people you know.

Hiring from within may also mean looking outside your own section to other departments in the organization. That can be beneficial, too, since you and many in your company may already know the staff member applying for your position. You can rely on "internal references." Since the primary reference will probably be another manager in your organization, you can expect the internal sources to be more candid than if you were hiring from the outside. Management personnel who have solid objectivity and sound evaluation skills can be very helpful, but you have to refine your own interviewing skills so you can make your own judgments as well.

Other employees and your human resources department can also give you much needed background on the person, letting you know if they're a good worker and a good fit for your unit, or whether they're someone best left in another area. Make sure you're not getting another leader's failures.

Also, take into consideration that if an internal candidate is doing a good job in a current assignment, you could let that bias your view. They may do a great job in another department, but be a terrible fit in yours. Make the judgment based on the job skills you've concluded are critical for success in your job, not on how a candidate's performed in another job. Still, you'll have more information than if you hired from outside the company.

Keep in mind there are risks to hiring internally. Some of your staff may be falling short of your expectations. Merely reassigning them may be like moving deck chairs on the *Titanic:* you won't save the sinking ship and you won't help your organization. If that's the case, you'd probably do better to get a transfusion of new blood into the company and hire from the outside.

Don't accept weak performers. If the internal candidates applying for your opening are mediocre at best, you need to consider outside hires. New, aggressive talent added to an established team of slow and average performers can energize the entire team. The impact of new energy can cause a team to find new life and vitality.

Of course, the new team member may also be influenced by the lethargic old team and become mediocre, but it's less likely.

Don't Roll the Dice Because Luck Is Against You!

How many times have you said, "I'm really not happy with this candidate, but I need someone to fill the job, so I'm going to roll the dice on this one"?

How many times was that a good choice? If you're being honest with yourself, the answer will probably be, "Almost never."

Every manager has made bad decisions like that, and unfortunately, many will make them again. Why? Because they're desperate and maybe a little panicked to fill a position.

No advice from this chapter can have a more immediate impact on your success than this: avoid quick fixes in staffing. You'd be better off hiring a temporary employee until you can find a good permanent replacement, rather than hire the wrong candidate. The negative impact of a bad apple on unit morale and organizational achievement can be so severe the recovery time will far exceed the delay in hiring the right person.

Live with the pain in the short run, and avoid the much greater agony of picking the wrong person, who ultimately will probably have to be fired. Think of the time, paperwork and headaches involved in giving an employee a pink slip. Be careful and don't take a chance on an obvious misfit.

You don't need to go outside the organization to find a misfit. You can make the same mistake when you promote someone from within your organization to a job which is completely wrong for them. That person may even be one of your better employees, someone you were convinced would do well in another position. But if you don't take the time to really talk to them, you may not discover how wrong a fit they'd be.

These "misplacements" may cost your organization—in multiple ways. Not only do these employees have the potential to fail to achieve your organizational goals, but their move into your division may mean their former department will suffer a performance drop because it's lost a good employee.

Your roll of the dice may create more problems than it solves.

A bad hire can negatively affect you personally, too. If your unit suffers from having a less-than-adequate employee join the team, you'll lose credibility. All associates in an organization want to have confidence in their leader. When you're a new leader, your staff will start out with a relatively unblemished opinion of your ability to lead. Each error you make demonstrates your humanness. But if you have too many errors, your employees will start to look at you as someone who's borderline incompetent.

Your people selection skills will get the first and most serious scrutiny because that speaks volumes about how you view people and what you expect of your staff. If you think your employees won't notice, think again.

Like it or not, as a leader, you're always on stage. Every action you take will be evaluated as an indication of your ability. When you make a bad hire and don't choose quality people with the necessary knowledge, skills and attitudes to deliver, you'll lose your employees' support.

As a leader, you can't afford to make too many mistakes. No pressure there, right?

There's a serious aspect to consider if you make a bad hire within your company: if the associate you promoted from within doesn't do a good job in his or her new assignment, their reputation and self-worth will be damaged. The individual may have been a top performer in his former department and was thrilled to receive a promotion into yours, but now he's going through agony feeling inadequate as he realizes the new job in your department is a bad fit.

Your bad hiring choice has put a quality person on an emotional roller-coaster and turned a winner into a failure. That's nothing short of a human crisis for the associate.

Now is when you really need to express managerial love for this person.

Decide quickly if it's a failed assignment, and, if so, reverse the decision quickly by finding a way to help the person recover. Maybe you can provide an opportunity for a positive performance experience by locating another job in the company which would use his skills rather than his weaknesses. Worse case scenario: you find this person another job in another company.

Whatever you do, do it quickly. Self-esteem is fragile and your sincere love for the person will best be served by helping them move

Work Leader's **Tip:** To Find Stars, Look to the Ground, Not the Heavens!

The key to having a winning team is to have great players. The New York Yankees keep winning because they have stars. Of course, the Yankees' owner pays whatever it takes to get them. Most of us don't have that kind of budget, so what you need to do is to find stars who don't yet think they should be paid a star wage. You need to be the talent scout who sees the greatness in a Babe Ruth before the Babe hits all those home runs. That takes lots of time, and probably some luck, but the payoff is huge. Find a person with raw talent, then find a way to encourage that person to be an outstanding performer.

Here are some qualities to look for to find the type of person who can become a star in your organization:

- A spectacular academic track record. Intelligence and discipline matter.
- Evidence of the ability to work one or more jobs and go to school full time. This shows a willingness to work hard in order to achieve a goal.
- A quality résúme focusing on measurable and quantitative results.
- Great verbal skills. There's almost no job where verbal skills are unimportant.
- The ability to write well. That's essential in almost every job.
- Evidence of job change motivated by a lack of challenge. You want commitment to success.
- A person with demonstrated skill and accomplishment in your field. Great experience and success matter.
- A reality-based candidate whose expectations and dreams are high. Someone who reaches and wins.
- Behaviors which show a high energy level and enthusiasm. High energy gets the job done.
- Evidence the person isn't satisfied with mediocrity. This defines the star mindset.

into a position where they excel. That way they can rekindle their confidence and self-worth. The longer you wait to correct the problem, the more you're going to cause the individual to lose self-esteem. Help them look for a way to avoid the embarrassment of facing peers who have witnessed their failure.

Unless you intervene, the associate's likely to be a casualty to himself and be a major loss to the organization.

The good news is if you make more good decisions than bad, your employees will probably view you favorably. If you find great new hires, either within or from without, those individuals will love their job, your existing employees will be glad to welcome a strong team member on board and you'll achieve your goals.

Find the Stars

If you staff your team with mediocre hires, you'll get average performance. If you staff with stars, you'll soar and peak performance will follow. There's no substitute for stars.

Organizations with winning performance records have a disproportionately high number of stars on the staff. You can have that, too, but it takes discipline and a commitment to never accept average performance when choosing staff. If you want to be a winner, you need to focus on hiring winners.

Loyalty to average performers may be honorable, but it's unlikely to create a winning organization. You have to love your quality associates enough to make sure the people who weaken the performance of the team are moved out. Love each of your staff members, but not to the exclusion or the detriment of peak performance. You have to love your team enough to select only the best.

Unfortunately, we all have a tendency to get comfortable with average performance. When somebody's meeting expectations, we normally are pleased, but we should always be striving to improve the existing level of performance. Good enough isn't good enough. General Electric didn't get to be the winner it is by accepting average performance. Toyota didn't get to be the quality leader in automobile manufacturing by accepting good-enough cars.

Your company or your section can't excel if its goal is to be average—and that's what you communicate to the staff when you accept average performance.

Every group of staff members will be made up of people who represent the best and worst. Even if you think your group overall is above average in performance, somebody's always going to be lagging.

You definitely want to keep your best performer, but you need to decide how you're going to help your worst employee, even if it means helping him or her leave. That's not cruel. You'll not only be helping them find a place where they can excel, but you'll also be setting the bar so your superstars can excel. Your average workers can either strive for improvement or drop out.

Group performance will attempt to rise to the level of your expectations and the example which your superstars are setting. But if you don't have any stars and your employees aren't of the highest quality, that journey's probably going to be long and painful, even frustrating.

It can be hard to hold on to stars, but there is a way to keep your best employees. Stars want to be around the best. Excellent workers strive for promotions which challenge them and offer them the opportunity to use and learn new skills. If you're really doing your job as a Work Leader, most stars will opt to stay with you and your company if there are other stars they can work with and if you provide them with enough opportunities for growth. Even if another company headhunts your stars and offers them jobs, they'll reject the other organizations' offers if they suspect they'll be working with less talented employees than they're working with in your department. They won't leave your company if they believe the other job's environment will be short on energy and high on mediocrity.

Build a team of stars and you'll have more fun, they'll have more fun and the organization will outperform its competition. That's what stars are all about—winning.

If you're a Work Leader of a professional staff, star employees are even more important because so much depends on their ability to be superior individual performers in their technical specialty.

"Outstanding firms are consistently able to identify, attract, and retain star performers; to get stars committed to their firm's strategy; to manage stars across geographic distance, business lines, and generations; to govern and lead so that both the organization and its stars prosper and feel rewarded," write Jay Lorsch and Thomas Tierney in their book, *Aligning the Stars: How to Succeed When Professionals Drive Results*. Lorsch, a Harvard Business School professor, and Tierney, chairman and co-founder of The Bridgespan Group, add, "These capabilities are what give great firms their competitive advantage."[18]

Case Study

Sarah was about to go home when she saw her boss Barbara walking toward her desk—not what she wanted or needed at the end of a terri - ble day. Almost every day had been bad in the six months since she'd taken on this new job. Sarah knew Barbara was going to give her anoth - er lecture about credit approval processing.

Barbara said, "Sarah, you turned down five more credit applications today which you should have easily approved. Honestly, I don't under - stand why you can't get it. You did such a great job as an application processor. This move to credit analyst should have been a snap."

"I still don't understand what I'm supposed to be doing," said Sarah. "I know you've taught me several times and I've read the book three times. I think I understand it. But when it comes time to complete the numbers analysis, I get confused. I never was very good at math in high school and some of this stuff I'm supposed to do is very hard for me."

What Sarah couldn't bring herself to say was she really hated work - ing with all those numbers. When she was processing applications, she loved the work. She loved talking to applicants on the phone and she loved writing letters to them. Her new work was boring. Even worse, she hated not being able to talk to clients anymore. She felt isolated and cut off from people.

"I loved my other position. It just didn't pay enough," said Sarah. "I wish I could get the same pay, but do what I did before."

"That's not possible," said Barbara. "We promoted you to this posi - tion because we had a crisis opening. We knew you were ambitious and would work hard to catch on. Were we wrong?"

Sarah thought for a minute, then said, "No, I'll work even harder and I'll get it right."

But deep down she knew it wasn't possible.

That was the moment Sarah decided she needed to look for a new job. This one was making her miserable.

Questions

1. Sarah's miserable. Why is she so unhappy? Could anybody have predicted the problem?

2. What should Sarah do? Is there a way out of her misery?

3. What should have been done to avoid the problem for Sarah and Barbara?

4. What should Barbara do? Can she save Sarah or is it inevitable Sarah will leave or be fired?

chapter four

DEVELOPMENT
The Good Get Better,
The Best Excel!

Your associates rely on your commitment to them and nowhere does that get tested and proven more often than when you're focused on their development.

This chapter is the central theme of your journey.

Your job is to commit time to developing people's abilities. If you're focused on their development, when you gamble on a new associate, that becomes an investment. But if you fail to commit, the gamble will frequently result in a loss.

"The basic role of the leader is to foster mutual respect and build a complementary team where each strength is made productive and each weakness made irrelevant,"[19] wrote businessman and author Stephen Covey in his book *Principle-Centered Leadership.*

The goal of a great Work Leader is to assign great people, then give them room. That doesn't mean getting out of their way, but rather giving them an opportunity to win based on their own abilities. It's allowing them to achieve success without giving them so much room they fail.

Think about it this way: some swim instructors like to use natural instincts to teach children how to swim. When they throw a young child into the pool, they figure what's most likely to happen is the child will briefly panic, then begin dog-paddling to stay afloat. A small number may continue to panic and start to drown, but no responsible instructor would allow that to happen. They'd immediately lift the child's head above water and save him.

Dog-paddling may keep a child afloat, but it's not swimming. Swimming is a skill which has to be learned, generally from someone who knows the proper strokes.

It's the same with your staff. The key skills required for success also have to be learned. Talented people will always find a way to survive, but that isn't the goal. You want them to *succeed*, not just survive. Left unattended, those treading water to survive may drown if they don't get help, even if they're strong.

If it becomes obvious a staff member is drowning, you have to save him. You have to use training and development as an investment in accomplishing your mission. By training, I mean providing your employees with structured learning about a specific subject, increasing their knowledge, skills or attitudes. Development is when you help your associates grow on a daily basis through things as simple and powerful as comments you make to correct their mistakes. Every interaction a Work Leader has with his associates should be viewed as a development action.

"Has the leader a right to mold and shape?" writes workplace psychologist Dr. Harry Levinson in his book *The Exceptional Executive.* "Of what use is aging, experience, and wisdom if not to be the leaven for those who are younger? Of what use is pain if not to teach others to avoid it? The leader not only has the right; if he is a leader, he has the obligation."[20]

Whether you hire the best people you can from outside the company or promote the most outstanding ones from inside your organization, you still need to invest in them because they're the ones who are going to be doing the work. Organizations invest in machines, computers, desks and buildings, but all too often they make a trivial investment in the most precious factor of production—people.

Think about your own case. Whether it was your first job or your most recent one, did you know everything on the first day of work? Obviously not. So what happened?

If you were lucky and worked for the right leader, you learned all about the job, perhaps even well before you started performing the required tasks. If you were even luckier, you learned from the leader each day on the job. If not, you made lots of mistakes and, with some persistence, eventually learned enough to get by. But if the company had made an investment in you, you would have been more productive faster.

Development is hard work. It requires a commitment of time and

Work Leader's **Tip:** Use Formal Training In Even The Smallest Unit

Your organization, whatever its size, should have some type of formal training experience for new associates, either an orientation program, or technical, sales or management training. If you don't have a formal training program, you're telling your workers training's not important and they may never be required to do those actions again. Any perception a new associate has that they'll never have to do what's being taught is dangerous, naive and foolish. Formal training doesn't necessarily have to take place in a classroom, but you should have a preplanned program, along with a set schedule of events and time frames. You should also have a deadline for completion, a set of specific learning outcomes and a way of assessing what's been learned, such as a test.

Here are some hints for a successful training program:

- Whenever possible, you, the Work Leader, should be the trainer. Your success is on the line.
- If you assign the training to another associate, be sure it's somebody who likes doing it.
- If you assign the training to another associate, make sure he's good at it.
- Provide your new associate with a copy of the entire schedule. Emphasize planning early.
- Explain what the expectations are.
- Use this three-step rule so they remember: 1) Tell them what you'll teach them. 2) Teach them. 3) Tell them what you taught them.
- Teach the concepts first, then the details. They need to know why and what.
- Test learning and reward success. If something isn't learned, teach it again, only differently.
- Have the associate teach you what he learned. That's a great way to test knowledge.
- Use lots of examples and practical exercises. You're not teaching theory. You want results!

money, along with the belief a better trained and developed associate is a better performer. Once again, love for the individual should be your driving force. If you really love your associates, you'll take the time to train them properly so they can learn to be more effective. That's good not only for your organization, but also for your employees. No associate wants to fail, but very few will truly succeed if you don't help them develop.

Most development begins with some type of training session for new associates. Some companies commit a large amount of money and time to have full-time staff conduct formal training classes. These sessions typically are designed to teach technical skills for a specific job and frequently give a general background on the organization and its business practices.

Other companies provide training to newly assigned staff through on-the-job training (OJT). In this case, the training function is held by the organizational leader or management and the training becomes a part of the day-to-day work flow.

Most people who enter new jobs get their training through OJT. Proponents of OJT argue the company saves the cost of a big training department, while new staff members learn from people who really know how to do the work. Of course, that depends on how good the employees are who are doing the training. If they're not exceptional, the new hires may only learn their bad habits and errors.

OJT Doesn't Mean *Omit* the Job Training

Unfortunately, for many new hires who are promised on-the-job training, they quickly find out OJT means *omit* job training. If that's the case at your organization, you're not doing your job.

If you've assigned Sally, the most qualified processor in your division, to train all new hires, but Sally's overworked, with stacks of files on her desk, and you're not checking to be sure the instruction is happening, your new hires won't get trained. Sally's going to be concentrating on clearing off the files on her desk so she keeps her job, not worrying about new people.

That means your new employee will probably have to learn most of the required tasks on his own. He'll pick up a little information here and a little there, spending a great deal of time trying to sort out what's correct and what's not. Is that really how you want your new hires to be trained?

Not only does it waste the new associate's time, but, worse still, he's going to be barraging the rest of your staff with questions, which is going to distract them and waste their time. It will also mean your department's going to have a lot of rework, correcting your new employee's mistakes. The poor new associate may even be unfortunate enough to have the big boss come around and conclude he's a slow learner or a bad hire. All because you didn't give the poor guy basic training.

Does your organization require on-the-job training? If so, is it your responsibility? Has everybody in your unit received the required training? If OJT isn't a required part of the organization, when was the last time you trained a new associate on the job? Did you make a plan and stick to it? Was it effective? Did the program actually help your associate grow into the job? All of these questions are critical because they focus on your responsibility as a developer. You can't ignore the critical role you play in the development of your associates and OJT is the key to the successful development of your associates.

With good planning and disciplined follow-up, OJT is not only helpful to your new associate, but also cost effective for your organization. When an organization takes an outstanding performer and makes that person a mentor for new hires, that's showing how committed the company is to high performance and to making sure new hires get off to a good start.

When you select someone to mentor new hires, make sure that person is patient, effective and enthusiastic about helping others. The mentor not only needs to fully understand the policies, practices and procedures of your organization, but also the ins and outs of the new hire's job. Mentors have to really want to help people learn and be willing to share their knowledge of your company. If the mentors you select don't have these qualities, you're going to have problems, with a strong possibility of failure.

You have to be committed to the concept of training. If you put more emphasis on getting the work out and neglect effective training, your department will constantly be in crisis mode. There's never any easy or convenient time for training and development, but you have to make the time if you're going to be an effective leader.

If you're not training your new employees, perhaps it's because

---

Work Leader's **Tip:** Have You Made These On-the-Job Training Mistakes?

If you find yourself making statements like these to your new hires, you're going to end up with poorly trained associates. Not only that, they'll probably also develop an attitude problem and their lack of training will end up causing you and your department problems in the future. Have you caught yourself saying any of these things?

- "Here's the Operations Manual. Read this and come back in three days."
- "I don't have time for you today. Go home and come back tomorrow."
- "I just showed you the basics. Now go read the manual to understand the details."
- "This manual's all wrong. We do it differently."
- "I know what the corporate policy is, but we changed our procedures. Don't tell corporate."
- "Here's a stack of work. Go give it a try."
- "I don't know how to do that, but we can figure it out later."
- "I know that's what Frank said to do, but it's not important enough to do every time."
- "I hate this job and I can't believe you'll like it either."
- "We did half of today's training. Let's just quit and get back to it tomorrow."
- "I hate training people. I'd rather be doing my own job."

---

you were never trained to be the instructor. It's not as easy as it sounds.

"Leaders do a lot of teaching—giving instructions, explaining new policies or procedures, doing on-the-job training. Yet very few leaders have received special training to carry out this important function," wrote communications expert and conflict resolution pioneer Dr. Thomas Gordon in his book *Leader Effectiveness Training*. "They don't appreciate how difficult it is to teach people effectively—it is more complex than most people think."[21]

Dr. Gordon makes the point that many instructors don't realize just how much people resist learning something new because it requires them to give up their familiar ways of thinking about or doing things. Learning requires change and that can be disturbing and threatening to some people, especially if they feel the instructor is demeaning and treating them like a child. That's why it's so important for the teacher to be trained correctly—so new hires won't feel belittled.

How you structure the training is critical. Focus on what it takes

---

Work Leader's Tip: How To Interest An Adult Learner

Adult learners can be either the best students or the worst, but the best way to ensure they achieve success is to avoid showing them how to do everything.

Instead, use the conference method, which is a combination of you explaining things and the other students participating in a dialogue about it. That way everyone can contribute their life experiences for everyone's benefit. Reinforce the learning by having all the participants do practical exercises.

Here are some additional ideas to turn the challenge of training adults into a great opportunity for learning and success:

- Use lots of "practical exercises" which feel like real life.
- Use real-life, hands-on examples.
- Have students solve a real problem or answer a real inquiry.
- Don't have adult students sit for long.
- Be prepared to be challenged. If you're wrong, admit it. If you're right, be tactful and don't hurt anyone's feelings.
- Act like a teacher, not a boss. That means be patient. Not all ideas will sink in quickly.
- Theory is for graduate school. Teach them what they need to do the job.

to be successful and tailor each session to the individual's current level of competence. Find out what your new associate already knows, then address the area of new information.

Do you have a list of all the required knowledge, skills and attitudes necessary to make each person a fully capable performer? If not, make a list of those and take the time to check with your associates to find out if you've missed anything.

Now you're ready to design an effective OJT experience. Without those first two steps, you'll lose the advantage of OJT which is specifically tailored to the individual. At this point, preparing a plan for each person not fully skilled will be easy and effective. Make sure it's structured along the needs and skills defined and make sure you're able to test how well they've learned and absorbed the information. You can do that with formal tests or more informally by asking questions during the training. You have to know if your associate is learning what you're teaching.

Classroom Training: You're Teaching Adults, not School Children

At some point, a new associate will probably endure some type of formal classroom training. Although we've said OJT is very productive, it's also true more formal training is probably going to be required. That demands a more intense, disciplined and controlled environment, like a classroom. There the trainers will have more control over the subject matter and be able to use professional teaching tools or techniques. It's more efficient because they won't be distracted with their own work.

That kind of classroom training puts everyone on the same page because it guarantees all employees will go through the same type of learning. That's particularly important if the subject matter is complex.

Does your organization have a formal training program for new staff members? Has every staff member in your unit been through the program? If not, why not? If it's because you've failed to get them there because the work load keeps you from releasing them, you're not doing your job. No matter how effective your OJT has been, getting your associates trained in the formal process will be critical to their success.

If you're doing the training, remember you're teaching adults.

Don't insult them or talk down to them. Not only that, but remember adult learners are more impatient with a classroom environment because they have the benefit, and the burden, of life experience. Most will probably be more eager for real-world applications rather

Work Leader's Tip: Are Teaching and Coaching The Same?

Teachers can coach and coaches can teach, but they're not doing the same jobs. Teachers tend to focus on knowledge, while coaches tend to focus on skills. When we teach people what to do, we're giving them knowledge. When we coach them, we're giving them the skills so they can use that new knowledge.

Good coaching means:

- Showing how to do a task
- Asking why someone did a task
- Observing what was done and making suggestions for improvement
- Helping with a task when it's too complex
- Praising success
- Encouraging risk taking
- Providing constructive and corrective feedback
- Teaching facts and knowledge when required
- Supporting failure with solutions
- Answering questions when asked
- Offering help without threat of criticism

Good coaching isn't:

- Giving orders
- Giving punishment
- Demanding success
- Giving instructions and walking away
- Withholding support
- Using emotional pressure
- Being intolerant of mistakes

than something conceptual. They won't always be receptive to new knowledge because most have probably completed all the formal education they intend to experience.

For example, someone who's worked as a medical lab technician for ten years has not only learned a great deal about the technical characteristics of lab work, but her interactions with other people have also shaped her view of her profession. She's learned how people react to the stress of a potentially serious illness, how they react when told good news about a loved one and how her peers react when they're stressed by an exceptionally long day of work. If you send her to a workshop on how to deal with terminal patients, she'll be coming to the class with real-life experiences which she'll use to evaluate your lesson plan. Even if she's very interested in learning, she'll have her own ideas about the subject. You're not dealing with an empty slate. She's drawing upon a wealth of life experiences.

Adult learners will challenge everything an instructor says. That's not because they're being recalcitrant, but because their experiences have formed the way they view life. Every time a trainer provides an insight which goes against their life experience or the conclusions they've drawn from it, adult learners will want to challenge that. If they've had significant experience, they can become down-right stubborn about learning new concepts or data. When there's a direct contradiction between the lesson and their life experiences, the learners are more likely to go with their life experiences.

That can be bad if their experiences drew a wrong conclusion. When you're training adults you have to distinguish between their valid conclusions, which resulted from their experiences, and their wrong conclusions. If their conclusions are valid, the adult learner may actually contribute important knowledge to the class, but if they're flawed, you as the trainer have to find a constructive way to help them "unlearn" their conclusion.

Another point to consider: they won't accept new ideas as meaningful if those ideas can't be put to a practical use. Tell a lab technician people are afraid of needles used to draw blood and you'll see a big yawn. Tell the technician the key to easing anxiety can be learned from the tricks used by magicians and the learner may challenge the applicability or value of the idea, but is more likely to listen to you. Tell the technician magicians are able to create illusions because they can direct the audience to a distracting event, which allows them to perform the trick, and the technician may now understand the concept. He may recognize a meaningful distraction, such as shaking the person's arm, could be the way to make a patient more relaxed before the needle's inserted.

The message here isn't adult learners are stubborn—just the opposite. Some of the most dedicated learning happens when adult learners are really motivated to absorb knowledge and skills which they know are required to achieve their dreams. Those aspirations help stimulate even bigger leaps of growth, personal improvement and development. Watching a motivated adult learner can be a thrill for even the most experienced leader.

Using practical applications of classroom learning is one of the great tools available to adult trainers. When in doubt, have adults do practical exercises and have them bring real-life problems from their job. Get them involved. Stay away from lectures and trainer-directed show-and-tell. Instead, have them do the show-and-tell.

Many times a class can be the better teacher than the trainer. Why let years of experience go to waste? Harness your employees' experiences to help the rest of the group learn. This kind of training requires careful planning and good control, but, if it's done well, it's a fantastic way for adults to learn.

A formal classroom-like setting can often be helpful in developing a work unit's staff. Practical exercises are a great way to facilitate learning and at the same time get management tasks accomplished.

For instance, after you teach your employees how to set goals and explain why setting expectations is so critical to their success, break them into smaller groups and separate each group. Then have everyone do goal setting for their own job and present that to the other groups for a critique. Their peers will probably be more critical, but more helpful to them, than if you'd provided feedback.

Coaching

Remember the old saying, "If the student failed to learn, the teacher failed to teach"? Your employees have the responsibility to understand and absorb new information, but you have the responsibility to do the teaching, so focus on creating an environment where the learners can find their own way.

You can try to tell an employee what to do, but you'll probably hit a brick wall because adults can be skeptical. Remember, you're coaching, not ordering people like a drill sergeant.

As a coach and mentor, you have to encourage your employees so they want to discover new things. Help them learn and provide them with the energy for self-development. Great coaches train the mind and the body to achieve more than the individual could have imagined. They inspire with energy, enthusiasm and love. They create an environment where people want to achieve. They also teach trainees how to achieve precision and excellence. Good coaches love, set expectations, assign talent to the right positions, develop abilities, evaluate performance, provide rewards and are constantly growing their own competence through self-improvement.

You have to lead your staff all day, every day. Developing your employees' skills is a daily routine, not something done for a couple of hours at the end of the day.

Each time you work on a technical task with an associate, that time is an opportunity to coach your staff. Each time associates have a positive experience, it increases the probability they'll learn. Each time you pass up an opportunity to help them learn, you've lost ground in the effort to achieve excellence from your staff and to meet or exceed your organization's expectations of your work unit.

To lead a peak performance organization, you have to commit the time to coaching your staff. Helping them grow may be your highest priority as a leader. When they grow, your unit's performance will grow and peak performance will be the end result.

With Love, Patience Can Coexist with Persistence

If you're a Work Leader, you probably got the job because you had high standards and expectations for yourself, as well as being a high-potential, high-energy performer.

Chances are patience isn't your strong suit.

When you became a Work Leader, you expected, or at least wanted, your staff to go into high gear, just like you do. But if they, instead, moved more slowly and less effectively than you do, you probably became impatient with them.

What you need to remember is their abilities, their current level of knowledge and their skill development aren't as advanced as yours.

If you refuse to understand they still have things to learn and, instead, keep showing excessive impatience with them, your employees are going to quickly get frustrated. If you don't control your impatience, they'll conclude you'll never be satisfied with anything they do. Your impatience and their frustration with your bad attitude could even lead to them leaving your organization in search of a more accepting and nurturing boss.

Small steps are a critical part of individual development. Small

---

Work Leader's Tip: When Do You Empower Your Associates To Fail?

As a Work Leader you can't sacrifice the mission of your unit, but you need to allow your new employees to have some time to try out the new skills and information they're learning—even before they've totally mastered them. So when do you take off the "training wheels," allow them to make their own decisions and possibly fail? You do it only when your unit's performance isn't threatened.

Consider the following examples:

- Give a machinist a task, specify the requirements and let him set up the run, then check the results.
- Give an accountant a ledger to reconcile and have another associate check it.
- Have a salesperson handle a prospect all the way through the sales process when it's not a major sale.
- Have a new customer service representative handle all calls during an hour. Monitor all the calls and give feedback.
- Allow a newly trained lawyer to write an entire brief, then provide an edit and critique.
- Allow a newly licensed and certified hairstylist to handle a customer, then give your input.
- Have an accounts-receivable clerk handle all the transactions for a day. Review the work the next day.
- Have a new teller handle all the transactions at a window. Check the balance at the end of the day.

victories are the key to large change. Seldom does the process of human development reflect a dramatic shift from old ignorance to new enlightenment. Most of us learn incrementally and find our knowledge gains result from adding together small bits of new knowledge.

That's the approach you have to take to develop raw talent—baby steps. Each hour of each day you should be helping your workers grow one step at a time. Rome wasn't built in a day, nor was your knowledge. It took time for you to arrive at your current level and it'll take time for your employees to develop as well.

The key to changing behavior—and that's what you're doing when you focus on helping an employee develop their skills and knowledge—is to never let up. Much of the change you're seeking won't occur if you fail to follow up on the effort. Your first priority has to be to reinforce the behavior you want and extinguish every behavior you don't want.

Just be prepared to start exercising some patience because your staff won't get the message 100 percent of the time. You'll have to repeat and repeat and repeat. Never assume a worker fully understands what you're teaching. Keep focusing them on the goal and reinforce they're successes. It'll pay off.

If you're like most Work Leaders, you've experienced a time when a new policy or procedure has been implemented. Most people don't like change, but there are a few employees who will always seem to stubbornly resist new methods. They've been doing things the same way for years and, even after you try to convince them the new methods make their work easier, train them and insist they implement the changes, for some reason they refuse to see the merits of the new ways.

That's going to reflect on you and the whole unit. If your workers won't implement the changes, you're going to start getting negative feedback from your bosses.

Obviously, you're going to have to show patience, but that's not going to solve the problem. You could be completely patient, but that won't guarantee they'll ever accept the new method. And if you order your employees to do it anyway, there are probably going to be a few who offer up passive resistance. That can cause a serious morale problem. You have to implement the change because if you don't merely to avoid conflict with some people, you risk failing yourself.

What you really need is "patient persistence." Understand your workers' emotional and habitual reluctance to change, but tenaciously focus on making sure the change occurs. The key to patient persistence is to stay focused on the goal of implementation while maintaining a softer touch.

Empathy for your workers can't degenerate into sympathy, but you have to recognize their sense of loss of control. It's a serious problem and has to be handled over time.

By giving persistent reminders, with a sensitive and loving tone in your voice and body language, each and every time you have an interaction with them, you'll ultimately convince them not only that you understand their concerns, but also that you're not going to give in to their resistance to the change.

You may also need to frequently sit down with some of your employees and go through the changed procedure yourself to learn firsthand precisely how it's impacting their jobs. Then you're part of the process and you can show the benefits from direct knowledge. All but the most recalcitrant worker will get the message and begin the painful process of compliance.

Empowerment and the Ability to Fail

No amount of mentoring, tutoring or classroom instruction can prepare an employee for daily on-the-spot, immediate decisions. But eventually, each worker will begin to synthesize the bits and pieces of the training. That's when you need to release the reins and give your workers the chance to make decisions on their own without consulting a rule book. That kind of empowerment doesn't mean you're ignoring the rules. It just means you're telling them they have the authority to act in the best interest of your organization. You're telling them you trust their judgment to make much the same decision you'd make under similar circumstances.

Empowerment is giving authority to act based on trust.

That's a very strong vehicle for learning and growth. It's amazing how well your employees will do when they know you trust their decisions. If you've hired the right people and you've taught them well, they'll rise to the occasion. Yes, they'll make judgment errors at times, but, more often than not, the lesson and the values you've instilled will prevail.

If you hold back your workers by not allowing them the opportunity to succeed or fail, they'll never mature to their full potential. The thrill of being the decision-maker helps all of us focus on making correct decisions. With solid development, coaching and mentoring, employees will succeed and be bolstered from that.

However, take note that empowerment can only happen when workers' development has been thorough. If they haven't been coached well, they'll fail. Some failures can be more devastating than others. At its worst, one worker's failure can cause an entire unit to plummet.

The best way to combat that is to make sure your people are all carefully and thoroughly trained. Then, when they're knowledgeable enough, allow them to make decisions which involve risk.

Ongoing Development

Not all development should focus on job skills. You should also encourage your employees' personal growth, not just as a benefit to them, but also to your organization. Associates who know and understand themselves have more time to know and understand their work.

Far too many staff members spend half their lives searching for themselves and the rest of the time just getting by at work. An employee can't be productive if his day is consumed with self-doubt or worrying over personal inadequacy. It's not your responsibility to fund such efforts to find inner-confidence, but it is an opportunity to encourage them.

Deciding how to encourage these efforts for personal discovery can be a challenge. On one hand, you have to avoid appearing to act like an amateur psychologist. On the other, you actually need to do just that. Sort of.

You're not a therapist helping people work through their personal identity and psychological well-being issues, but, in many ways, you are a diagnostician. You have to be able to recognize when psychological challenges are having a negative impact on an employee's performance and, as a result, your entire team.

Because the diagnosis to help resolve your worker's problems is a sensitive and difficult matter, get all the professional help you can.

This is one of those times when consultation with your superior is probably the best advice. If your organization has a human resources department, go there for help. If the problem is major and severe, it may be necessary to have an organizational process which refers the individual to a therapist or a social service agency or even to a private-sector support, such as a minister or a counselor.

If you have a relationship with the worker or he discusses the problem with you, then you might be able to suggest he seek help. It's imperative you not damage your working relationship by appearing to interfere in his personal life. Getting professional support in handling this type of situation is always the best course of action.

What responsibility do your staff members have for their own development? Have they created their own development plans? Have you asked them to write out those plans and to commit to accomplishing them? Have you reviewed and approved them? How do you decide what additional training or development your staff requires? Do you have those programs already established? If not, you should create a program which can be used as a general development tool for the entire unit, not just for one or more staff members.

Your commitment to supporting continual development of associates should also extend to broadening knowledge beyond whatever's required for the day-to-day tasks. A course in art history may have very little to do with your work environment, but it can have everything to do with the development of a person who appreciates aesthetic beauty. In turn, it can influence an employee's ability to appreciate the value of the organization and its support of the arts in the community. The same could be said for a course in biology, which can help an individual appreciate the need to preserve the environment. In turn, it can help the associate recognize, and even get involved in, the efforts of the organization to preserve the environment at the workplace.

Seldom does a learning experience go to waste. You should encourage general educational development. If your organization can afford the expense, the company should subsidize advanced education, as well as encourage learning in any formal or informal setting which will help your employees grow. Don't just *allow* your employees to self-improve, *encourage* them. Expanded knowledge helps them grow.

On the job, consider allowing them to learn tasks they don't need to know and cross-train in other areas. One day that knowledge may have a profound impact on your ability to fulfill the organization's needs. Today's seemingly extraneous knowledge may lead to tomorrow's promotion from within. Let the B clerk learn about the A clerk's job. Someday you may need another A clerk. The added cost of satisfying the intellectual curiosity of an associate is trivial in comparison to the cost of ignorance.

Workplace improvements can and should come from your employees. Their increased knowledge and skills will enhance their ability to contribute to positive changes within your organization. Encourage them to speak up and express their ideas through suggestion systems, quality control circles and other means of participation. Harness their power instead of stifling them. Their growth can enhance your organization's growth.

What if you have staff members who have received all the training your organization requires, but they're still not performing to expected levels? What kind of learning experience could you develop which would make a real difference for them? Why haven't you done it? If you could do anything you wanted, how would you develop or train your staff members?

Weak performers may well be the result of inadequate training and development. They offer a clue as to why a development process has failed. That educational training, whether it's for skills or other knowledge, is somehow failing your staff and should be the first place you look to consider implementing a change.

Create a list of the shortcomings of your weakest staff member, then create a development plan which will provide a way to improve the weak employees' job performance. Compare the plan to the training and development plans already in place and, if there's a disconnect, talk to the training department about the problem.

Continued growth is essential, even when excellence has been achieved. Keep the pressure on and push your associates to continuously improve. Complacency is a serious problem for a developing associate. The need for continuous improvement is never greater than when staff members are fully comfortable with their current level of knowledge. As they lose the thrill of growth, they'll become bored and may decide to leave to find something more exciting. Those who stay will settle into a comfortable rut and, inevitably, their performance will deteriorate or, even worse, they'll fail. Standing still isn't possible. The choice is either move forward or fall behind.

Focus on the Stars

As challenging as it can be to help your weakest employees, your toughest challenge will be with your strongest ones. While you're spending much of your daily routine helping your underperforming workers become a success, trying to modify their behavior and even playing amateur psychologist or social worker, you're neglecting your strong employees, leaving them to fend for themselves.

I learned this lesson from a candidate for a senior management position in my organization. During the interview, I asked him to tell me about a time when he'd taken a problem employee and helped that person become an excellent associate. His answer

---

Work Leader's Tip: Look For Holes In Your Employees' Knowledge, Then Fill Them

It's imperative you teach every employee in your unit how to do his or her job and do it well. The organization relies on knowledge. Pass on what you know by making it easy for your staff to learn. Here are a few tips:

- Don't make fun of ignorance. That only discourages questions. Remember, you were ignorant once yourself.
- If your associates know what you do, then you'll have time for other tasks your boss needs you to work on.
- Make it fun for your staff to learn. Reward their learning.
- Most associates want to learn more, so give them new challenges every day.
- Knowledge is power. When your staff knows they have power from their knowledge, your own power will increase.
- You'll never get promoted if you're the sole source of knowledge.

shocked me. He said he'd never been successful in transforming a truly weak employee and he'd never really spent much time trying. His mentor had advised him early on that he should spend almost all of his development time (eighty percent or more) with high-potential people and help them become great, leaving the weaker associates with only the remaining twenty percent of his time.

Since this idea violated everything I then believed about leadership, I didn't hire the candidate. As fate would have it, my very next meeting was with one of my managers who'd already taken up too much of my time the day before because he'd made a serious managerial mistake. I spent an hour with him explaining why his decision was simply wrong and destructive to the organization, but he couldn't understand why I was making such a fuss over the issue.

Right after that meeting, my best manager came to me, asking for help with a problem. At this point, I only had five minutes before I had to meet with my boss. By the time he laid out the problem, it was time for me to leave.

As I was going out the door, he said to me in a rather frustrated tone, "Gerry, I really needed help and you couldn't give me five minutes. I guess I'll have to find somebody else to help me."

I knew I'd let him down. He was my best manager and deserved better. That night I was forced to look at myself in a very painful way. The candidate I'd rejected had been right. That's when I began to change my thinking about leadership development and what it takes to reach peak performance.

You're not going to achieve peak performance with mediocrity. Your company may be better than another company, or your unit may excel over others, but you won't achieve peak performance until you have stars dominating your staff and you're spending the majority of your time helping them grow.

The key to this concept is to remember a star may not start out as a star performer. A star is a person who has the *potential* to become an outstanding associate, but may not have arrived at that level of achievement—yet. It's a person who has long-term potential, so don't rule out anyone based on their current performance.

Focusing your development efforts on your stars isn't an elitist philosophy. It's simply the best use of your time. When you help a worker develop into star performer, you haven't only served yourself well, but also you've served the individual and your organization as a whole. Ten minutes of helping a potential star to do a better job will pay greater dividends than ten hours with an employee who's underperforming. You shouldn't write off the unsatisfactory performer, but you have to make sure the star gets the benefit of your leadership first. The investment will have a phenomenal return.

Ask yourself which staff member is your potential star. Have you adequately trained that person? Is that person performing at his or her capability? What can you do which would make that person your company's highest performer?

Armed with the answers to these questions, sit down with that person, tell her you want to develop a plan for advancing her growth, then give her the opportunity to participate in developing the plan. You'll get her attention and your commitment may even get her energized.

Share Your Knowledge: The More *They* Know, the More *You* Grow
In order to be a great teacher, a leader first has to know how to share. That means being willing to give your employees exclusive knowledge. For many leaders, knowledge is power and, by not sharing with their associates, they protect their own position and assure continued job security.

However, as a Work Leader you're the key to your organization's ability to replicate itself because you hold the detailed knowledge. Your work unit is where the projects are completed. It's where the parts are made, the assembly is completed, the research is accomplished and where the breakthrough in new products occurs. Someday you may move on, but if your unit doesn't have a leader, it will fail in the core mission of your enterprise.

The inevitable result of successful development is the workers you're mentoring will no longer need you. Do your job well and you won't be needed. Your entire concept of leadership has to include the willingness—indeed the commitment—to train your associates to eventually become leaders themselves. This transfer of leadership is essential for the survival of an organization.

Your ability to transfer knowledge to your associates is the true measure of your ability to lead. When they've learned from you and can function without you, you've liberated them and yourself. You'll be freed to focus on your own success. However, if you continue to guard your knowledge jealously, you'll thwart your own development. This is because only when your organization can succeed without you, can you expect to move on to your next assignment.

If you do your job well, you'll be growing leaders, not followers. This means as you develop your associates, you're developing your organization's future management. Many leaders fail to develop staff to replace them. The two tragedies of that are: (1) you'll never have anybody to replace you as you look toward your next promotion; and (2) your organization will never have the staff to grow their existing responsibilities.

If your employees' growth into leaders threatens you, you aren't a true leader. Always groom not only your successor, but also your boss's successor. Try hiring and developing people who are better than you are. What happens is remarkable. They'll bloom and you'll get even better. That's a win-win-win situation. They win, you win and the organization wins!

Case Study

Stan had been a trainer for leadership development for nearly two years and he was under a lot of pressure. Now the vice president was coming. His last visit had been a disaster. The VP had asked Stan how the pro-gram had changed since he'd started teaching it and Stan was stunned with the question.

"I haven't changed it at all," he said, "I was told an expensive outside consultant developed the program five years ago and top management didn't want it changed."

At that point, Karen, his boss, gave him a look which made him feel worthless. Stan had a very uncomfortable feeling he was in trouble, but he didn't really understand why.

Karen said, "I didn't think Stan should tamper with the successful program and, besides, he doesn't have the program development experi-ence it would take to modify the program. I think I'm the only one in the section who has the knowledge and I simply haven't had time to teach him. Besides, that's really my job and not his."

At that point, the VP said to Stan, "I'm disappointed you haven't taken the initiative to modify and update the program. I thought you had a bachelor's degree in adult education and a master's in executive leadership. That seems to me to be more than enough background, Karen. You should work with Stan so we can better utilize his education - al background."

That little incident created quite a problem for Stan. For the next three months, he kept trying to get Karen to work with him to show him what he needed to do to make program modifications.

Karen's answer was always the same: "Stan, I don't have the time. When I do, I'll do the changes myself. Just concentrate on being a good trainer. I'll worry about program development."

Karen started becoming more upset with Stan and less willing to help him grow. All the program development reference materials were in her office and it was clear she wasn't going to share her knowledge.

When the VP announced he was coming back for another visit, Stan knew he'd be asking him the same questions. Unfortunately, Stan would have the same unacceptable answers.

If he told the truth, Karen would be even more upset with him. If he didn't tell the truth, the VP would think Stan was one who was lazy and unwilling to improve himself.

He figured there was no way he could come out of the meeting look - ing competent.

Stan became very stressed out thinking about the VP's upcoming visit, so much so that he came down with a bad cold and missed the meeting because he was home sick.

Three days later, he quit.

Questions

1. Why did Stan quit?

2. Why didn't Karen work with Stan? Would Karen have been able to improve Stan's performance?

3. What could Stan have done to fix the situation so he'd get what he needed to develop his skills?

4. Do you believe Karen has a responsibility to further her own improvement? What should her boss be doing to help her?

chapter five

EVALUATION
Be Definitive and Make Employee Judgments

A quick review: we started with *Love* for our employees, established *Expectations,* made the right *Assignment* and then worked at *Development* of our associates. Most readers would probably guess *Evaluation* of performance is the logical next step, but if it's so obvious, why is evaluation often ignored, postponed or forgotten?

How many times have you yourself waited a whole year for your annual performance appraisal, only to discover you haven't been doing the job your bosses wanted you to do?

Evaluation Is Hard Work, But With Love It Might Be Less Stressful
Nowhere is the concept of love for your employees more important than when you're evaluating them.

It's often the most personally challenging and potentially painful aspect of being a Work Leader. Nothing you do can be more helpful—or more damaging—to your workers. Do evaluations well and they can be exhilarating for you and your team. Do them badly and they can be devastating for everyone. No wonder this step is so frequently avoided.

Many leaders find evaluations one of their least enjoyable tasks. Even giving performance reviews to outstanding performers can be just as hard as doing reviews for unsatisfactory performers. There's no way around it: evaluations are hard work.

Most leaders want to receive meaningful and timely performance reviews about their work, especially if they think they've done a great job. You'd think that would motivate them to do the same for their associates, who also want feedback, but most avoid the task because they don't want to endure negative feedback sessions with subordinates.

Five Reasons Why Leaders Avoid Evaluations

You know you have to do evaluations, but, if you're like most leaders, you tend to avoid them at all costs. Some of the reasons may be:

1. Most of us simply don't enjoy being judgmental of others, especially people we work with every day. We like to avoid such conversations because they create tension.

2. We don't want to cope with employees who disagree with their evaluations. Workers are likely to agree with any positive feedback you give, but they're just as likely to disagree with negative feedback. The stress is intensified if the performance

---

Work Leader's Tip: Ask Yourself These Questions And See Why Appraisals Are Tough

- Have you ever been surprised by a remark on your annual performance appraisal? Why? What did you do about it?
- When was the last time you got feedback from your boss? Was it positive feedback? Was it negative? What did you do about the feedback? Did your boss discuss how you could improve?
- Think of your worst staff members. When was the last time you sat down with them, gave them a formal performance appraisal and discussed their performance? What happened?
- Think of your best staff member. When was the last time you gave that person any feedback at all? What was it about? What was the outcome?
- What happened when you had your last performance appraisal with a staff member. What was the result of the meeting? Has there been any change in performance from person?

review is tied to pay, as it most often is. Even an outstanding performer, in a meaningful and honest evaluation, should receive some negative feedback, but, instead, may receive an all positive performance review if the Work Leader doesn't want to cause tension. The result is the issues which need to be addressed for change are ignored. That can cause problems later.

3. In order to evaluate, you need criteria. That means you need to have expectations you can compare to the job performance. If you haven't made the expectations list specific and measurable, you have a very difficult time measuring against the benchmark. The worse you are at setting expectations, the more you'll worry and procrastinate when it comes time for evaluations. Ultimately, the result will be an evaluation which is weak or inadequate, compounding the tension which already exists whenever negative feedback is given.

4. The documentation required for an evaluation takes a lot of time most leaders would rather spend getting the work out. Often you're required to complete forms which make you record factors you weren't really tracking or you thought were irrelevant. You may wish you'd focused on those items, but now it's too late and you're going to have to fake the results.

5. You may be convinced the people who are doing a good job know you think they're great and evaluations for them are a waste of time. You want to tell them everything's fine and not much more. More times than not, you won't give them an evaluation, but, instead, will make a quick comment and give them a salary increase. You think everybody's happy and you can go back to work.

All of these reasons reflect a failure to assure performance.

"Everyone has peak performance potential," wrote management expert Ken Blanchard in his book *Leadership and The One Minute Manager*. "You just need to know where they are coming from and meet them there."[22]

The problem is you can never meet them there if you never tell them where they are. How can you develop your employees if you never give them insight into their current level of performance?

If It Was Simple, Everybody Would Be a Leader

Giving a performance review to an outstanding performer can really

---

Work Leader's Tip: Get Yourself Ready For Tough Feedback Session

When you're preparing yourself for a feedback session, here are some things to consider which might help you keep your resolve:

- Great Leaders evaluate performance.
- It's part of your job.
- Procrastinating only puts off the inevitable.
- Employees' performance has to be good or your unit's at risk.
- Your employees won't know how to improve if you don't tell them about areas they need to work on.
- Workers deserve your honest feedback on their outstanding performance.
- Your associates deserve better performance from those workers not performing well.
- If an employee's behavior is abusive and unacceptable, tough love may be your only solution.
- If an associate isn't right for the job, he or she is probably just as miserable as you are.
- If an associate's shown a lack of integrity or trust, or their performance is negatively impacting other in your unit, you need to fire him or her immediately.
- If an associate has alienated your customers many times, you need to have them pay the bills.
- If you've worked with an employee for at least six months, and he or she has done nothing to improve, you need to let them go. You've probably spent too much time trying to help a hopeless case. Others in your unit need your time more.

make you feel good. For most of us, praise is a great deal more fun than criticism. It's only when we're forced to give strong, highly critical and negative feedback that most of us wish we could ask somebody else to do it for us.

One senior executive routinely did just that. He'd give all the positive reviews himself and leave the negative reviews and even firings to his director of human resources. This man was incapable of facing his responsibilities as a leader. He always wanted to feel good and couldn't face the difficult task of confronting another human being with the honest and caring truth. Worse still, he convinced many people in the organization he was such a warm and caring person that he couldn't bring himself to hurt anybody. What a fraud. If he'd truly cared for his associates, he'd have recognized it was his duty to do everything he could to help them succeed, even if it meant telling them something they didn't want to hear.

Loving people requires helping them, even if the truth is painful. Those with no understanding of their weaknesses are living in a fantasy world. It's your duty to help your associates deal with their own shortcomings, as well as help them understand their strengths. Just as in a manufacturing environment, you can only improve the process by understanding its weaknesses. Improvement can't happen if you don't know what needs to be improved and, without improvement, there can be no excellence.

Remember: you're not trying to create capability, you're working to enhance it. Don't waste your time on the hopeless, but where there's hope, give it a real commitment.

"People don't change that much," wrote business consultants Marcus Buckingham and Curt Coffman in their book *First, Break All the Rules*. "Don't waste time trying to put in what was left out. Try to draw out what was left in. That is hard enough."[23]

Even Daily May Be Too Seldom

If you're only giving direct, formal evaluations and performance feedback once-a-year, you may be compounding the problem. That's too long to wait. For one, it's unfair for your associates and secondly, it's not beneficial to your organization.

Evaluation has to be an activity which is tied to the individual's daily performance, not the convenience of a process.

You can't expect associates to know what you don't tell them. Either positive or negative messages about behavior or performance has to be communicated at the time of the event, not a month or a year later. How can you expect change if you make no attempt to inform associates about their performance?

Annual reviews don't work to the benefit of the associate or the organization.

"The semiannual or annual appraisal is not a particularly efficient stimulus to learning...It provides 'feedback' about behavior at a time remote from the behavior itself," wrote the late industrial psychologist Douglas McGregor in his book *The Human Side of Enterprise.*

McGregor was a management professor at Massachusetts Institute of Technology and former president of Antioch College in Ohio.

He continued, "People do learn and change as a result of feedback. In fact, it is the only way they learn. However, the most effective feedback occurs immediately after the behavior. The subordinate can learn a great deal from a mistake, or a particular failure in a performance, provided it is analyzed while all the evidence is immediately at hand. Three or four months later, the likelihood of effective learning

---

Work Leader's Tip: Give One-Minute Feedback Immediately

Give one-minute feedback whenever it's obvious an associate's behavior was either exceptionally good or obviously inappropriate. Here are some things to consider for your session with your employee:

- Do it immediately. Waste no time.
- Make your comments clear and crisp.
- Be calm, but firm.
- Refer directly to what just happened.
- Give positive, warm and friendly feedback if your employee did an excellent job.
- If it's negative feedback, make it firm but gentle.
- Above all, make the session short and focused only on the event, not a history lesson on other events.

from that experience is small. It will be still smaller if the superior's generalized criticism relates to several incidents spread over a period of months."[24]

If you fail to reinforce desired behavior, it will eventually disappear and if you fail to punish undesirable behavior, it will continue. Behavior will persist until an individual understands the core reasons for its existence. If you allow an associate to go without an honest evaluation of behaviors and performances, you'll have failed the love test.

If you really love your associates, you won't allow them to drift with no idea as to how they stand. Unfortunately, too many leaders fail their associates and give them, at best, severely delayed feedback.

Make Certain You Really Have the Associate's Attention

When you give feedback, make sure your employees actually hear you. Most of us have a difficult time receiving feedback and, when we do, tend to only listen to what we believe or want to believe, especially positive comments.

Think about the last time you were asked to list your strengths and weaknesses. In all likelihood, you did a good job on the strengths and not so well on the weaknesses. The weaknesses you listed were probably qualities you actually considered strengths. Most of us have a difficult time admitting to real weaknesses and, if we do, we generally find a way to excuse them. We tend to do the same with evaluations.

Think about the last time you asked one of your employees to tell you their weaknesses. He or she probably answered with comments like, "I'm impatient when others fall short of the goals," or "I set standards some people think are too high," or "I work too many hours."

Maybe your employee really believed these observations could be viewed as weaknesses or maybe they'd learned to only mention things which appear to be weaknesses, but which, in reality, only make them look like better employees. In most cases, impatience is good when it looks for excellence, high standards are great when they challenge associates to achieve excellence and hard work is a positive when it reflects an associate's commitment to achievement. In short, the comments really reflect pride, not weakness.

Most people have a tendency to block out bad news because they

---

Work Leader's Tip: How To Get And Keep Their Attention

Try some of these statements when you need to get an associate's attention.

- For those who are direct: "Frank, I want you to know this is a formal feedback session."
- For the receptive type: "Joe, I have some thoughts which might help you improve."
- For the chronic failure: "Barb, we've talked about this problem before."
- For the serious event: "John, you've just made a serious mistake. We need to talk."
- For the worrier: "Sally, you've asked me to give you feedback."
- For the rude one: "Kim, I'd like to discuss your outburst."
- For a victory: "Stephen, you just did a great job. Thank you."
- For an obvious error: "Mark, I'm very concerned about they way you handled that."

---

only want to hear only good things. They don't want negative things said about their behavior, so, even if they hear them, they don't process them.

That means if you're talking to someone like that, they may see you moving your lips, but they're blocking out everything you're saying. The sound hits their eardrums, but doesn't make its way to their conscious mind for processing. How many times have you shut out a speaker's words by simply turning off your attention? Your associates will do the same to you.

Have you ever given a worker frequent negative feedback only to have them later tell you you've never told them about their failings? It's frustrated and bewildering, isn't it?

Try this technique: tell your associate she should listen carefully because you're turning on the "counseling switch." Then walk over to the light switch on the wall and turn on the bright ceiling lights. This bit of drama frequently works. By the time you sit down at the table, your associate will be clearly focused on what you have to say. You need to do whatever it takes to get their attention.

For those workers who either don't get the idea or are offended by your "game," try other methods. Do whatever it takes to get their attention. Make sure your worker understands you're serious and you expect him to hear what you're saying.

When you give negative feedback, always announce you're about to begin a counseling session. This suggests what's about to occur involves the associate's performance and has to be remembered. Make sure you always use the person's name. Always make the feedback session private, not in front of other associates.

Talk about Behavior First

Whether your worker's performance is superior or unsatisfactory, you have to give them feedback, but remember all individual performance is a function of behavior.

If employees come to the job with severe behavioral limitations, their job performance will be negative. If they come to the job with weaknesses, but substantially improve their job performance, give them positive feedback and tell them you care about their success.

What people are and how they behave can make a difference in your expectations of them. Focus on qualities such as: their intelligence, their ability to reason, how they think logically, the way they articulate ideas and function under stress, as well as how they relate to other people. Observing all those qualities will help you define who your workers are and how they'll perform. You need to know them. It's not enough to say, "You did a great job." You need to understand them as whole beings.

A good way to do this is to use "trait reviews." These aren't report cards on behavior like children used to get in elementary school, but they do have one critical resemblance: they give feedback on characteristics of behavior which can influence an associate's ability to perform. The goal has to be to focus on results, on performance compared to expectations.

It's equally important to give feedback on those traits which help or hinder success. If an associate has trouble developing working relationships with her peers, that weakness is going to have a major influence on her ability to achieve results in almost any organization.

If you give her effective feedback, counseling and developmental support, she's more likely to become a superior performer.

If you choose to avoid this sensitive psychological issue, it's the same as withholding your support of your employees. You'll be cheating them of your leadership. Remember, you can make a huge difference in your workers' lives and impact their futures. If you really love them, you'll try to help them acknowledge and deal with their shortcomings.

Of course, how effective you are will depend in large part on how receptive they are to what you're saying. Your performance is critical. If you give feedback in a sensitive way which shows you care about them, their feelings and their ego, plus understand what they're going through, there's a much better chance they'll hear you, acknowledge their weaknesses and accept them as things which need to be changed. Only when your workers hear you in a non-defensive way will they begin to acknowledge their problems and work with you to find and implement a solution.

But, if you preach at them and moralize, there's a ninety percent chance they'll tune you out. Making speeches may make you feel better, but it will probably make your associates reject what you're saying. Get preachy and you'll alienate them.

Don't avoid discussing with your employees their development because you think psychology isn't your job. Evaluation is hard work, but it's what you have to do if you're going to do your job well.

Helping to make winners isn't always easy, but it will always be rewarding for a leader who begins with love.

Now that we've established the proper tone you should have, let's get into the trait review itself.

Trait Reviews Are Tough, but They're Great

Never tell associates you're evaluating them on their personal traits. Performance evaluations should be based on your associates' achievements, the results of their daily work, not their behaviors, but the trait review gives the associate an opportunity to correct issues which are affecting their job performance.

The content of a trait review follows a simple structure, but it has to always be part of a comprehensive review of the associate's performance. Never do a trait review without tying it to a performance evaluation. The goal is to give workers an opportunity to see their performance can be tied to their personal traits.

You probably think about the behaviors and traits of your friends, family and even casual acquaintances all the time, but seldom tell them what you really think of them. That's because it's not an easy task, so you avoid it. You may even be afraid if you didn't handle it well, they'd never speak to you again.

However, as a leader, it's your job to observe, then evaluate your employees' behaviors and traits. You can't avoid it. You have to discuss with them how their behaviors are affecting their job performance. Results at work are almost always tied to behaviors.

Amazingly, many workers think no one's aware of their traits, probably one reason they don't make an attempt to change them. That's why you have to discuss those behaviors with them—so they know you know. You see what they're doing, good and bad. If they know you've observed wrong behaviors, that just may be the impetus to inspire them to deal with those issues and begin making changes.

True, it can be difficult to tell your employees how you perceive them, but if you handle the trait reviews well, they can be a positive experience for you and your workers, as well as lead to their professional growth.

If you don't handle them well, your discussions can quickly turn into arguments. When employees object to your feedback and challenge you, a simple way to deal with that is to acknowledge you know you may be wrong, but explain to them that's why you're talking about it. Tell them you're only trying to better understand them so you can all find a way to improve job performance. Tell them you'll spend some more time thinking about it. This acknowledges you could be wrong without saying definitively you are. Being right isn't the issue. Giving your associates the information makes it possible for them to understand you have a certain perception of them.

The Process Is Critical

Always begin a trait review with an introduction explaining to the associate you're not a psychologist, but rather a leader who has great interest in understanding her so you help her grow and improve. Then give a general review of the categories you'll discuss and the reasons for discussing them.

Consider covering the following five key characteristics during an evaluation: 1) your employees' mental skills; 2) their emotions; 3) their knowledge of their job; 4) their relationships with others; and 5) their future career prospects at the company.

Let's take a look at each of these.

1. The Mind

Mental skills surely affect job performance because most jobs today can be viewed as "knowledge worker" positions. How the individual uses their mental skills is critical to their ability to learn, as well as execute job functions. In this part of the trait review, give your associate feedback on abilities, such as:

a. Their ability to achieve effective reasoning.
b. Their problem solving skills.
c. Their systematic and logical thinking.
d. Their ability to employ analytical skills to create new approaches.
e. The speed with which the associate learns new ideas.

2. The Emotions

Emotional stability and control is a critical requirement in any job environment. You and your unit have to be able to rely on others in the unit over an extended period of time and in a variety of situations. In this part of the trait review, give your associates feedback on characteristics, such as:

a. Their ability to maintain emotional control.
b. Their ability to deal with constructive feedback on work performance.
c. Their commitment to work.
d. Their self-confidence.
e. Their ability to deal with change and stressful situations.
f. Their ability to avoid personal problems which could affect on-the-job performance.

3. The Knowledge

Every associate has to be able to demonstrate a core knowledge and understanding of the work they're doing. In this part of the trait review, you'll give your associates feedback on their job knowledge, such as:

a. Their understanding of business principles in general.
b. Their understanding of specific work unit activities.
c. Their knowledge and understand of the organization as a whole.
d. Their knowledge of the specific jobs they're assigned to accomplish.
e. How they apply that knowledge to their required jobs.

4. The Relationships

Any person in the workplace has to ultimately deal with co-workers in order to be effective. In this part of the trait review, you'll give your associates feedback on abilities, such as:

a. How they work with colleagues.
b. Their capacity to develop a sound working relationship with you, the boss.
c. Their commitment to working as a team member.
d. Their capacity to become a leader.
e. Their commitment and capability to develop cross-organizational relationships.
f. Their capacity to effectively handle customers, vendors or any other professional relationships and how that impacts their job success.

5. The Future

Any associate who's to be a star in an organization will need to be able to think about the long haul. In this part of the trait review, you'll give your associates feedback on abilities, such as:

a. Seeing and understanding business growth opportunities.
b. Their willingness to develop plans for improvement in the organization.
c. Their commitment to establishing plans for personal development.

When you take the time to discuss these key characteristics, you demonstrate to your employees you're committed to feedback. By sharing these thoughts, you give them an opportunity to understand how you and your organization perceive them.

Love Means Honesty and Candor—not Brutality

Giving effective feedback is hard work, but taking it is, too. Hearing negative words about behavior or performance is painful for any individual. Because you're in a position to give feedback, attempt to couch the words in the most appealing fashion you can.

If you've been exposed to any formal sales training, you were probably taught you should always deal with negatives in a sales situation by attempting to focus on the positives instead. You were also probably told you have to make yourself communicate in a positive fashion in order to get an order from a resistant buyer. Training like that gives you all the more reason to walk carefully through the minefield of feedback.

The recipient of constructive feedback in an evaluation session will be that "reluctant buyer," so you may think you should always focus on the positives as you've been trained. However, that's not the best approach in all situations. Sometimes you do need to provide candid and direct insight, rather than try to mask the truth and spare people the pain of confronting their weaknesses. If you do mask the truth, your employees may then come back and tell you later that you never told them they were doing anything wrong. Yes, you can be *too* nice.

Still, in spite of the need to be direct, there's no reason to be brutal. Statements like, "That was stupid," or "You failed," are cruel and confrontational. That kind of language will illicit a strong reaction. The idea isn't to devastate your worker.

Try a statement like, "I think you have some areas which could be improved." This approach shows you believe the worker can fix the problem and the short-term failure can be overcome. It provides hope. You're showing your feedback is constructive for the purpose of improving the employee's performance. Your goal should be to clearly and directly communicate the evaluation, but you have to continue to take all actions based on your ability to love.

"There are three L's to keep in mind when delivering a review:

Work Leader's **Tip:** Prepare Before You Evaluate

- Chose the one person in your unit who needs a counseling session most and prepare an outline of the discussion you'll have with that person.
- Describe what you plan to do to deal with the most unsatisfactory performer in your unit. Create an action plan for dealing with that person. Be specific about what your expectation is for the result of your plan.
- Practice the session. Role play with yourself in order to build your confidence.
- If the counseling session wasn't successful, prepare a brief on a final session where you'll terminate the person.

Level, Listen, and Leave yourself out,"[25] writes engineer and former CEO of Intel Corporation Andrew S. Grove in his book *High Output Management.*

"Level" means to be frank and honest because your credibility is on the line. "Listen" means just that. "Leave yourself out" means try to avoid the bias of your own thinking. It's not about you. It's about your employees.

Write Objectively Because People Believe What They See

Using the written word is another way to deal with your associates' natural tendency to rationalize they're doing an adequate job. It's a strong dose of reality. Seldom does anybody fail to get the message from written documentation. That's true for positive evaluations, as well as negative ones.

But that's not the only advantage. What you write out is more likely to communicate the essence of your message because writing helps you sort through the key concepts you want to communicate. In addition, you're much more likely to be careful about what you say if you put it in writing. It can also help you clarify your ideas or, perhaps, even change them.

Many of us don't enjoy writing and may need to be convinced writing evaluations isn't a waste of time. Typically, organizations require a written performance appraisal. The document you're discussing may satisfy the organization's expectations, but it's not for the organization, it's for you. It's your guide to help your employees improve. You'll be a better leader if you give better evaluations.

Giving your associates constructive feedback is only half the responsibility. There's one more critical step: you have to commit yourself to influencing their behavior. Of course, you can't make the changes in behavior and performance. Only your employees can do that. Your communication to associates has to place the responsibility for their behavior and performance squarely on their shoulders.

All too often, your employees will look to you to either explain their difficulties or to solve their challenges. Frankly, at times, you may be the cause of the difficulty, but in the vast majority of cases, this retort is simply an expression of frustration. The associate knows the problem exists and puts the problem right back on you. Obviously, you have to consider carefully any assertion the problem is your fault, but, in most instances, you shouldn't accept that burden. In the final analysis, individuals are responsible for their own behavior.

Get Plans to Fix the Problems and Follow Up Consistently

Evaluating your employees is useless if they don't decide to make a change in their behavior or performance. They have to have a plan of action, as well as show they're committed and making an effort.

Employees can't just saying, "I plan to do a better job," or, "I plan to be a better person." Planning is deciding what the goals are and how to know if they've been achieved. It takes defining specific actions which will lead to change, laying out a timetable for doing them, establishing checkpoints along the way and creating a mechanism to assess whether the actions and results are on track to accomplish the goals.

All of that is hard work, but associates who have a sincere desire and commitment to improve will continue to show how disciplined they are about their behavior. They'll find ways to show they're making the necessary steps toward success.

If they don't show commitment, most workers will fall well short of their original goals and you'll be having the same evaluation discussion later.

That's where a Work Leader comes in. You have to follow up on your evaluations. You can't make changes in your workers or enforce their commitments, but you can support them and there are several actions you can take to help them achieve success.

First, offer to help each employee develop a plan and set goals. By being involved in this process, you're clarifying and enhancing your role as leader. Further, if an associate hasn't been able to establish a format for the plan, you can help create a structure. After it's completed, offer to provide feedback on the plan.

One of the many values of you taking part in your employees' self-improvement plans is that it gives you the opportunity to validate your evaluation feedback. If each worker's plan addresses the issues you raised in the evaluation, then, at a minimum, you can say you've succeeded in communicating the need for improvement.

If each worker's plan doesn't address the issues, then you have an opportunity to refine the process before he or she wastes weeks or months focusing on the wrong issues. It's hard work. You have to have love and commitment to help all your employees improve and reach their fulfillment.

Next, ask associates how they're doing on their personal improvement plans. It sounds simple, but you merely asking can have a profound effect. When you ask a question, your staff listens. When you listen to their answers and respond appropriately, your staff is affected. Never underestimate the influence you have on your employees. You're the single most important person in their daily lives. Your interest in them and your questions to them make a powerful impact.

Third, acknowledge when your workers improve. When you recognize improvement, you're reinforcing positive behavior.

We'll look at that more closely in the next chapter.

Case Study

Fred was on his way to put in another boring day at work. He'd been at the company for about ten years and in his current job as a supervisor for exactly twelve months.

"Maybe that's why I have a meeting today with my supervisor," he thought. "I'm probably due for a salary increase and she wants to tell me what it is."

Fred had had a tough adjustment to this last promotion. He'd kept the problems to himself, but he really didn't like being a supervisor. He liked the people, but he just didn't like giving orders.

His boss, Sally, had been there for a long time and all the people on the staff were afraid of her. Fred had tried to become friendly with the staff, but Sally told him during his first week on the job she didn't toler-ate "fraternization."

Fred didn't say anything to Sally, but he thought that idea was silly and he continued taking coffee breaks with his staff. After many months, he'd gotten to know them well and liked them very much. The only prob-lem was many of them weren't doing what Sally expected them to do and Fred couldn't get them to perform.

"Maybe that's what Sally wants to talk about today," he thought. "I hope so, because I'd like her advice on what to do. We really don't talk very often."

When Fred walked into Sally's office to start the meeting, she asked him to close the door.

"I've never seen her ask anybody to close the door," he thought. "I wonder what's up?"

"Fred, you've been here a year," said Sally. "I need to give you your performance review. I don't know any easy way to say it, but it's just not working out. I've given you a full year to get the section in line and it hasn't happened. Contrary to my instructions, you've fraternized with the staff and your performance shows why it's a bad idea. You've missed all your goals and your staff is working at the worst productivity level in the entire department. Your evaluation is unsatisfactory and I'm going to have to let you go."

Fred thought his heart was going to burst out of his chest.

"I had no idea you were unhappy with my performance," he stam-mered. "What can I do to make it up?"

"Nothing," she said. "I've talked to personnel and they're waiting for you to out-process. Please give me your keys to the files and take your per-sonal belongings out of your desk. Report to personnel immediately. I wish you the best."

Questions/Discussion Points

1. How would you evaluate this performance appraisal? What was right? What was wrong with it?

2. Fred was surprised by what his boss was telling him. How

could he have been surprised? Wasn't he listening? Was he simply not very smart?

3. Was Fred's boss wrong? If you think so, what did Sally do wrong? How would you counsel her on her leadership?

4. Do you think Fred has a cause for legal action against Sally and the company?

chapter six

REWARDS
The Way to Obtain Optimum Behavior

At a very early stage in my managerial career, I walked into the office of a new boss and saw a sign on his wall which read, "An organization elicits the behavior it rewards."

This man ultimately became my most important mentor and the message on his sign has stayed with me ever since.

A dog behind an invisible fence learns to not go outside the boundary because he gets an electric shock when he crosses it. By the same token, he learns to sit on command when he's given a treat for doing it correctly. In short, there are two ways to learn—one through threat or punishment and one through reward.

Although we're far more complex than dogs, the same principles of learning can apply to us. The message in this chapter is "be positive." Although punishment has some value, the value of rewards is far greater. You learn what you should be doing by being rewarded for the behavior.

Early in life children learn the word "no." As they explore new things, their parents often try to protect them from harm by telling them "no." But as a Work Leader, you need to break the "cycle of no." Every time you think of the word "no" as an answer, try a positive version of response. Focus on what *to* do, instead of what *not* to do.

Negative Feedback Creates Fear and Fear Creates Flight

Using rewards to reinforce desired behavior is better than using punishment to eliminate unacceptable behavior.

The reason is simple: punishment can lead to serious negative reactions resulting from a fear of failure. Give adults the opportunity to be given an award for outstanding performance and they'll focus on doing what it takes to achieve that goal. Tell adults they'll be fired if they fail to meet a goal and, in all likelihood, their focus will be on avoiding failure rather than striving for success.

Fear can motivate, but it can also paralyze. If you fear something

---

Work Leader's **Tip**: Try The Positive First

Instead of: "No, you may not have the day off."
Try: "I'd rather you take off next Thursday. Will that work for you?"

Instead of: "Don't leave that box in the middle of the room."
Try: "Could you please put the box in the corner? It'll be safer for all of us."

Instead of: "I'm very unhappy with the quality of your assembly work. You're going to have to stay tonight for another two hours to fix the re-work problems."
Try: "Yesterday you had great quality on your production. I'd like to compliment you on that and ask you to help me learn why today's was so much less. Maybe you can find the problem and that way you won't be forced to stay overtime to rework all the problem pieces tomorrow."

Instead of: "You've been behaving very rudely toward your associates for several months. It has to stop. If it doesn't, you're going to be either transferred or terminated."
Try: "Joe, I was very pleased just then when you spoke nicely to Frank. That's the way I'd like you to treat everybody. If you do, I think your relationships with the other associates will improve and you'll have a chance to be considered for promotion a great deal sooner."

Instead of: "Sally, stop doing that. It's the wrong way."
Try: "Sally, here's what I'd like you to do. This is going to save you a significant amount of time and energy."

enough, you'll spend your time trying to avoid it, which is why achieving a goal because of fear won't always ensure success. An associate may respond to a negative feedback session with an immediate surge of adrenaline-driven energy, but he may also feel long-term anger. That can destroy effective learning and, ultimately, lead to resentment and resignation.

Fear at first causes a normal reaction of flight. You fear, you flee. But running from fear generally only makes you tired and, in some cases, can even lead to a denial of reality. It's a mind game we can play with ourselves. When you're afraid, you deny reality, hoping what you fear can't happen. You figure if something can't happen, then you don't have anything to fear. Therefore, you're safe.

Your employees may run from problems the same way in their work life. If they can convince themselves they don't really have any problems, they'll ignore them. Even the best adjusted have the ability to ignore problems in the hope they'll go away.

If you create a fear in them that if they fail, they'll lose their jobs, they may assume you don't really mean it and, instead, will ignore the problem.

Another reason people freeze when confronted with fear is they don't know what to do to succeed. They become immobilized and don't think clearly, not because they're trying to avoid work, but because they don't know what to do. They're afraid to take any action for fear it'll create failure. Signs of this problem happening can range from staring out a window to absence from work for extended periods.

Another type of reaction to fear can be a physical or mental shutdown. The body gets strong messages from the brain something is wrong and reacts in a psychosomatic way and becomes ill. The medical community is acutely aware of the mind-body connection. Those in holistic medicine recognize emotional events such as intense fear can trigger very serious illness. These illnesses aren't just in the mind. They're real, physical illnesses which can destroy a person. These reactions can range all the way from stress headaches to heart attacks, from rashes to severe immune system deficiencies.

In short, fear does push people, but leading by fear can cause your employees to experience negative psychological and physiological problems. Why would a person who loves others create this type of "dis-ease"? Although punishment is sometimes necessary, it has to be used sparingly and only when rewards fail to deliver results. Unfortunately, punishment frequently fails as well with people who haven't responded to rewards.

Work Leader's Tip: Watch Out For Misleading Rewards

Here are a couple of examples of how the correct intent can lead to the wrong result:

The intent: To motivate an associate to increase output at his work station by providing an incentive to speed up production.

The tactic: Tell the associate he can go home as soon as he finishes the assembly of the last twenty units on his work station.

The result: The associate speeds up the process, completes the units and leaves one hour early. However, the units now have a defect rate three times higher than the worker's former output and five times higher than his unit as a whole.

The intent: To improve a weak employee's performance by offering an added incentive to meet the quality standards of the unit.

The tactic: Tell the worst performing worker if he achieves customer service satisfaction standards, he'll get a day off of his choosing.

The result: The associate achieves the improvement in performance and is rewarded with a day off. However, the best performing associate finds out about the other employee's reward and is incensed and insulted. He needs a day off, too, to take an ailing child for tests, but he wasn't offered that incentive and has already used up all of his days off to care for the child. He starts looking for another job because he thinks the company doesn't appreciate his work.

At times, punishment is the only option, but it always carries the risk of adverse reactions. When somebody makes a serious error, your first action may be negative feedback. If your machine operator endangers the life of a coworker or your clerk makes an error which results in a $1 million loss, you're obviously going to have to give some negative feedback, even though your employee will probably react badly.

No reasonable Work Leader would hold back from the emotional reaction of a first class scolding, but the key to managing this negative feedback is to follow up with constructive corrective action. Turning a negative into a positive is necessary if you want to provide a real developmental experience.

Sometimes You Have No Choice but to Be Negative
Every Leader has abandoned "rewards only" leadership more than once. At times, the only possible action is a negative action. It's

Work Leader's Tip: When Using Financial Rewards, Use These Questions To Decide What To Do

- Think about the last salary review you did and the conversation you had with your staff member. Was the salary increase a good increase by your standards? If so, did your staff member appreciate it? Did the salary increase actually reward performance? Did it encourage that person to do even better? Has the person done better since the increase was given?
- Does your organization have an incentive system which rewards top performers? How does it operate and how do you apply it to your staff? Has it worked to recognize performance? Has it worked to encourage performance?
- Make a list of the top five financial rewards you plan to use during the next six months to reward performance.
- Do you believe the associate whose performance you're going to reward is "money motivated"? How can you make that decision? What happened when you last gave the associate a merit raise? Have you ever used a financial or cash reward to reinforce behavior in your workers? How did it work?

Work Leader's Tip: Plan For The Right Reward

- What is your plan to catch the correct behavior?
- Have you trained your associates to know what the right behavior is?
- Make a list of five non-financial rewards you'll use to reward performance on the spot when you catch somebody doing something right.
- Make a list of each person in your unit and beside the names indicate what's most important to that person. On the same list, identify something you could do for each individual or something you could give him or her as a reward for accomplishing a specific goal. Also, list one thing you think you could hold out to them as an incentive reward for reaching a goal.
- Describe the one reward you've received which was the most powerful incentive for you to continue performing at an exceptional level. Would it apply to anybody in your unit?
- Create a list of those programs you'd like to see your organization create so you could use them to motivate or reward your staff. Make sure at least half are programs which would have little or no money being given to the staff. Rank the list in order of your most desired.
- Write a detailed plan for getting your organization to implement one of the programs you listed.

natural to expect you'll get a negative reaction in return, so make sure the advantages outweigh the impact of negative reaction.

Fear and anger, the natural reactions in response to a criticism, can energize or enervate. Assess the potential result if the associate has an unfavorable reaction to your negative feedback, then decide if you can live with the consequences. As mentioned earlier, negative feedback probably is best reserved for times when you've had no real success with other attempts.

The real issue here isn't always related to the situation or to the associate involved. It may also be related to your prior behavior. When a tough boss, with a reputation for being critical, gives a strong piece of negative feedback, it may simply be viewed as just another incident, or it may be viewed as one incident too many. On

---

Work Leader's Tip: Giving Rewards Is Almost An Art Form

Cash rewards usually are effective rewards, but you'll be amazed at how effective non-cash rewards can be, also. Give employees things which are symbolic of their success and can be seen and admired by others. You'll almost always enhance the associates' self esteem. Try some of these suggestions for how and when to give rewards:

- A praising comment
- Flowers
- Candy
- A trip to Hawaii
- A note saying, "Thank you"
- A phone call saying, "Good work"
- Public approval
- Comments in a meeting about an achievement
- An e-mail containing praise, with a copy to the HR file
- A party in the person's honor
- A pizza party for the entire unit
- Lunch
- A cup of coffee at break time
- A visit to the person's desk to tell him, "Great job"
- A formal letter to the file noting extraordinary performance
- A handshake
- Some marketing material with the company logo, such as a pen, letter opener, sweater or tie
- Golf balls for a golfer
- A trophy for Associate of the Month
- A framed certificate of appreciation which hangs in the person's workspace
- A $100 on-the-spot bonus for something extraordinary
- An item from the organization's formal recognition program

the other hand, when a normally mild-mannered, quietly positive leader turns negative, the change will probably be strong and full of surprise and dramatic influence.

Your associates will expect you to be upset when a truly horrible situation develops. Remember if you don't identify a problem, you can't help people improve themselves. For this reason, even though you want to focus on positive feedback, it's also essential your associates understand where their weaknesses are.

Negative feedback, or a focus on failure, is inevitably a part of even a positive approach to changing behavior. Don't recoil from identifying weaknesses just because you're trying to focus on the positive. You can't allow the "be positive" message to prevent you from improving your unit.

Rewards Will Reinforce Behavior—Good or Bad

Organizations do elicit the behavior they reward, whether the behavior is good or bad. Contain the negative impacts by making sure your rewards, explicit and implicit, are focused on the behavior you view as good.

Let's consider a few simple examples.

Imagine an organization has an incentive system which rewards the sales and marketing departments by paying a flat commission on all sales over $1,000. The range of pricing for the products is $500–$25,000. Let's also assume the profit on a $25,000 item is thirty times greater than the profit on a $1,000 item. Obviously, the company would like to have the sales force sell as many large-ticket items as possible since it makes more money on them. Although the incentive structure will encourage sales over $1,000, you can be fairly sure the staff won't pay much attention to selling items with a higher profit margin since the incentive offers no extra reward to them and $1,000 sales are likely to be easier. The company is encouraging sales, but not the ones it really wants.

Let's consider another example. Say a company has an open-door policy with employees. If they have a problem with their supervisor, they have the right to take the issue to the next higher level of management—and are encouraged to do so. Many very fine companies have such policies and they can be quite effective at giving employees meaningful "escape valves" for legitimate supervisory problems.

Let's say the company has had the policy for three years and it seems to be working to everybody's satisfaction, except in one department. In this section, several supervisors have complained to the human resources department, saying the policy substantially undercuts their ability to manage. The director of human resources is concerned and conducts an investigation.

He finds there are ten times as many complaints in that department as in any other in the company. On further investigation, he discovers when the department manager receives a complaint, he always overrules his lower-level supervisors. In other words, the complaint is always resolved in the employee's favor.

It's possible every supervisor in that department has a leadership problem, but it's more likely the manager has created the problem because he rewards each complaining employee by always agreeing with his or her complaint. Over time, his employees have realized if they complain, they get their way. Therefore, they figure it's to their advantage to always complain.

As you can tell in each of these examples, it didn't take long for the associates to "break the code."

In the first instance, they figured out how to make the most money using the easiest way. In the second instance, they concluded they can have anything they want just by making a complaint up the chain of command. Both organizations elicited the behavior they rewarded. The only problem was the behavior was undesired.

The behavior of management in the first example isn't too typical. Most organizations will realize their incentive plan needs to be adjusted to encourage high-profit sales.

The second example is the most frequent mistake leaders make. The policy of that organization probably has safeguards built in, but its execution is a leadership responsibility. The manager in the one department is rewarding undesired behavior, in spite of a sound policy.

Leaders often do this without recognizing the impact.

You do it when you allow an unsatisfactory employee to continue in a job long past the time you should have taken adverse action. You do it when you promote the wrong person. You do it when you allow a person to come in late almost every day without any disciplinary action. In each of these circumstances, you reward the wrong behavior by allowing it to continue. All your employees will get the message and will begin to exhibit undesirable behavior.

Like it or not, all our decisions are on stage for everyone to see. If your associates see you promoting people they know are lazy, but who have personal charisma, they'll conclude the way to success is to be a nice person who goes home early. Pretty soon you'll see your entire staff racing to the door at 4:30 p.m. every day.

It's important to give rewards to the best employees who are exhibiting the proper behavior.

"Recognition of accomplishment (and the lack thereof) is an essential form of feedback," writes former Under Secretary of the U.S. Army Norman Augustine in his book *Augustine's Laws.* "To reward poor performance or neglect outstanding performance is like placing the controls for each separate half of an electric blanket on the wrong side of the bed."[26]

If you reward wrong behavior, you're sending all the wrong signals to you employees.

Cash Always Has a Benefit, but Less Than You May Realize
Financial rewards are a positive reinforcement for behavior. In fact, most Work Leaders consider cash as king. Every survey researchers have done has financial rewards as a useful factor, but virtually no surveys provide conclusive evidence they're the most important.

When you look to reward associates, you'll always have financial rewards in your quiver, but it shouldn't be the only arrow. That said, never ignore financial rewards. They do matter and should be used when appropriate.

Catch Them Doing Something Right
When you housebreak a pet, the key to the training is to reward or punish behavior quickly. In the same way, you have to catch your associates doing something right and reward them for it quickly. They, too, will remember the correct action a great deal better if the reward is on the spot, rather than substantially delayed.

The same goes for errors. It makes no sense to give an admonishment six months later. Do it immediately.

In the United States, we're not a society focused on patiently waiting for long-term feedback. We tend to want our feedback immediately, not later. When we look for rewards, the same is true.

Given this reality, you, as a leader, need to look for ways to reward positive behavior and results. Look for small rewards, as well as large ones. If a person you've coached on interpersonal skills comes to the office with a particularly pleasant demeanor and takes the time to be nice to a colleague, you should take the time to reward that behavior, right then and there.

If a sloppy worker does a particularly good job of cleaning up his workstation, reward him immediately. If a secretary you've coached about a lack of persistence finds a document she's been searching for the last few days, give her a reward right then. If a salesperson closes a sale he needed to make his goal for the month, reward him.

In every respect, catch your associates doing something right and reward them for it immediately. You'll be amazed at the impact.

Use Praise, not Just Money

How should you reward your associates? Remember recognition is far more powerful than monetary rewards. Of course, it's important to pay people what they're worth and, often, what they're worth changes as their performance improves.

Compensation isn't irrelevant, but it has much less of an impact than most leaders expect. People will do almost the impossible if they think they're appreciated and if they're being led by a person who cares about them.

Praise can be an art form or it can be a waste of time. When associates do the right thing or get the right result, they need to know the leader noticed. But noticing isn't enough. Be sure you communicate your approve of your employees' performance and tell them to continue achieving that same success in the future.

The real issue for a leader is to know when and how to reward. Make sure you pick the right time. You should always find a way to reward for success when expectations are achieved. It's particularly important to reward those efforts which result in successes where failure existed before, or when a major milestone has been achieved.

Always try to reward or praise right after an employee's success.

Case Study

Laura's boss Barbara screamed out to her, "I need to talk to you!"

Laura had heard those words before and they always gave her a headache.

"Here we go again," she thought. "Another tongue-lashing."

Before she could see what Barbara wanted, the phone rang. Laura had been waiting for a callback from an irate customer and wanted to take the call, but, given her boss's tone of voice, she decided to go see her first.

Barbara noticed Laura ignoring the call and, before Laura could say anything, she said, "You know how we're trying to improve our customer service rankings. Letting calls go unanswered is clearly not great customer service. And that's what I want to talk to you about. I got another com plaint call about you, this time on your phone etiquette. Laura, I can't understand how this happens. I've talked to you about this problem sev eral times in the last year and you don't seem to get the message. The last time I put you on probation and gave you a thirty-day warning. That seemed to get your attention. But within another six months, you did it again. I'm getting fed up with your inability to learn. What do you have to say for yourself?"

By now, Laura was beginning to have another one of those spells her therapist called an anxiety attack. She started to feel weak, her breath ing became rapid and she knew she'd soon start hyperventilating. Her fear was so severe, she felt she was going to pass out.

Barbara looked at her and said, "What's wrong with you? You look awful."

Laura could barely catch her breath long enough to say, "I'm having an attack. The doctors warned me about them. Please help!"

Barbara tried to calm her, but she kept getting whiter and whiter. Panicked, Barbara started shouting at people in the office to call 911. Fortunately, one of the associates, Carol, knew how to handle hyperven tilation. Carol rushed to her desk, dumped her lunch out of a paper bag and put it over Laura's mouth. After a few minutes, Laura began breath ing more normally. The crisis seemed to have passed.

Laura went back to her desk. A couple of hours later, Barbara came by and asked her how she was feeling.

"Oh, by the way, I got two letters complimenting you on your cus tomer service today," said Barbara. "I thought you might want them. I hope you feel better tomorrow."

Questions / Discussion Points

1. What is Laura's problem? Can she fix it herself?

2. Is Barbara a good leader? What defines her leadership?

3. Is Laura a problem for Barbara? What should Barbara do about Laura?

4. If Barbara is a problem, what should she do to be a better leader?

5. Did Barbara do well to give the letters to Laura? Did she get the maximum benefit from act? How could she have used them better?

chapter seven

SYSTEMS
How Structure Can
Free the Creative Mind

The previous chapters focused primarily on activities you execute as a leader and how they directly impact your staff's behaviors and performance. In this chapter, the focus is on the unit, how it performs its role and, more importantly, what you have to do to structure the activities of the unit as a whole.

The word "systems" is used to describe the structure a leader establishes to assure the unit achieves peak performance. It's a variety of activities coordinated in some way to accomplish a functional objective.

A company's systems are its organized standard operating procedures. They're the structure which, together with leaders, employees and other resources, provide efficiency in order to achieve the company's desired results. Without these systems in place, the workplace would be in chaos, but they have to be established with a keen sense of the role love plays in leading. You can't ever allow systems to become more important than your employees, to be placed above them in any way. That dehumanizes your workers. You always have to remember you're leading human beings, not machines.

More than 100 years ago, engineer Frederick Taylor began advocating industrial efficiency and scientific management which called for employees to do repetitive work in a very mechanical and routine way, like machines. Managers began accepting that model and it's continued, even to today. The average worker is still expected to do repetitive tasks under the guise of efficiency.

However, there's one thing to remember: your staff members don't get turned off at the end of a day. They're people, not machines. Even if they do run a "system," such as a machine, or even maintain it or program it, they're still human beings. As a leader, you have to create a systems environment with your employees in mind. If you lose the human connection, you'll be merely an overseer, not an effective leader.

Systems Support Leadership

It's important to keep the systems principle in the proper perspective. Systems support your core principles. They don't stand alone and they don't take precedence over leadership activities. Systems are a necessary condition for success, but, remember, whatever you do, you should always care about your employees.

There was a time when those in the academic and business communities became so enamored with systems and quantitative methods they started dramatically de-emphasizing the role of human behavior in the leadership function. This intellectual blunder led to a generation of people in charge who thought intellectual and analytical capability was all they needed to succeed. That generation, many of whom are in senior executive positions today, changed the organizations they led—and not for the better. Many of the illnesses in organizations today can be linked to that blunder. They ended up alienating their workers. Much of employees' dissatisfaction is a result of the organizational leadership failing to understand the necessity of leading employees with love as they manage systems.

Never forget the role of systems: they're in place to help you and your staff. They introduce time-saving efficiency, which then allows everyone to devote more of their time and minds to creative endeavors. Use systems to your benefit, but don't become a slave to them.

If a system becomes your primary focus, your organization's priorities are likely to be lost in the tiresome trivial administrative tasks, better known as "administrivia."

The Law of Administrivia:
The Greatest Barrier to Leadership Success

You have to do administrivia to keep your organization running, but that trivia can really bog you down. Many of the tasks are fairly easy to do, but they'll sap your time like a leech.

Most leaders dive into them to get them out of the way, usually to avoid trouble with the boss, then find they don't have enough time to do more productive work which might require more brain power. If you're stuck doing administrivia, you won't have time to be a manager.

That's not to say administrivia is useless. In fact, much of an organization's success depends on things like that. But if those are the only activities soaking up your time, you're not going to be an effective leader. Real leadership takes time and energy, but administrivia will suck up all the oxygen in the room, leaving you too little to function for your other responsibilities.

It can get even worse if you do it well. Your boss may gleefully realize you can handle all administrivia and dump more on you, leaving you even less time for productive ventures. Your "urgent" jobs may not be that essential to your mission, merely something your boss finds easier to ask for. Your job is probably many hours beyond a forty-hour "full-time" position already, so where are you supposed to find time for administrivia?

"The typical manager has more than enough to worry about," wrote psychologist and management consultant Saul Gellerman in his book *Management by Motivation*. "His typical solution is to arrange his problems in order of priority, deal with the ones he has time for, and just ignore the rest. In other words, that which is urgent gets done and that which is merely important frequently doesn't."[27]

What's the solution? If most of your time is spent doing tasks other than the ten leadership principles outlined in this book, you're wasting time. Being a good leader is your main goal and objective, so concentrate on that first, then deal with your administrative tasks by using planning, organizing and control to handle your administrivia work flow. Find a way to make sure they don't take up all your time—either through designating a specific time of the day to deal with those things, or only allotting yourself a certain amount of time. Whatever it takes to organize that part of your day, do it so you can spend the rest of your time as a good leader to your team.

Don't excessively focus on administrative systems. Instead, commit to your employees.

Systems Thinking: the Obvious Is Often Ignored

Every action you take has a consequence and every consequence causes another action.

MIT professor Peter Senge in his book *The Fifth Discipline* advocated using the "systems thinking" method or group problem solving within an organization. Senge said in trying to evaluate issues or solve problems, you have to consider interrelatedness and interdependence.

With systems thinking there are virtually no linear, unlinked events in the workplace. Almost all actions or analyses will lead you to the connection of a series of actions which then loop back to the beginning.

Not only does "every action cause an equal and opposite reaction," every action also probably starts five other actions, some of which will come back to the initiator of the initial reaction. Eventually, virtually all straight-line processes loop back to the beginning of the process and impact the beginning point.

For example, when you turn on your shower, the first water to come from the tap is relatively cold because it's been sitting in the pipes unheated. If you turn on the hot and cold water at the same time, the first flow will be cool to lukewarm. If you turn the hot water up to full capacity to increase the temperature, eventually the hot water will dramatically increase the temperature and the water will be too hot. The result will be you'll turn up the cold water to cool down the flow again. However, there's always a delay in the adjustment's impact on the flow and you have to compensate for delay in order to gauge your next move.

Unless you stop and think about what's happening, you could spend a long time reacting to water flow changes which never get a chance to fully adjust before you start making another adjustment.

However, if you realize what's happening, you can wait for the water to adjust and then determine the impact of your last adjustment. When you do, the time it takes you to end up with a comfortable water temperature is dramatically reduced. The system has a delay and you have to look at the entire system to get the desired result.

You can adjust behavior using the same kind of systems thinking. When you're dealing with human behavior, you're dealing with complex systems. You have to know and understand taking one action won't always have a simple, linear result. One action can precipitate a reaction from your associates, which then creates a whole new workplace situation. You're then forced to take other actions, or behave in a way which reacts to the new situation.

In a theoretically linear world A may cause B and then B may cause C, but in real life, often there's a next step where C impacts or "causes" A. This looping action reinforces the original action, so, once you've put the sequence in place, the results will reinforce the first action and intensify the result, maybe even to the point of "unacceptable results."

An example of this might be: (A) a serious counseling session with your associate indicating she's being too critical of her peers; which then causes (B) your associate to respond immediately by dramatically reducing her communications with her fellow workers; which then causes (C) her fellow workers to continue the mistakes the so-called "critical" worker was catching because now the initiative to give associate feedback has been dramatically reduced. With the reduced communications, the fellow workers sense a withdrawal by the "critical" associate and they dramatically curtail communication. With this series of events, the less feedback the "critical" associate gives, the higher the likelihood she'll stop offering feedback to her fellow workers altogether. Overall, the mistakes will actually increase because now the corrective feedback from the "critical" associate is missing. Over the long run, stopping the feedback would doom the company if there's nobody to pick up the issue.

Consider an opposite, but similar, situation: an employee offers critical feedback, causing a second associate to take some action to fix the problem. If the first associate continues her high level of negative feedback, the second associate may continue attempting to resolve the issue, but, eventually, may respond negatively to the ongoing critical feedback. Changes in the process may temporarily fix the problem, but the overreaction could result in increased tension which eventually causes the team to fall apart. The negative feedback strains associate job satisfaction, causing the entire group to become estranged from the process and, perhaps, even from each other.

The lesson is: nothing you do creates only one reaction. Your behaviors have a multitude of impacts and you have to be sensitive to the possibility that what you do to, or for, your associates will eventually have an impact on everyone. Not only that, but it'll impact how you act during the next stage of the process. It's not only a rippling effect, but also a boomerang returning to its source.

Another example of this could be the use of love and caring in the workplace. If you decide you're going to be a "loving boss" and take action to behave in a different (loving) way to encourage one of your associates to respond positively, she might interpret it another way. In fact, she could begin exhibiting a completely different behavior you weren't counting on. She may feel a sense of comfort and confidence that she can't, or won't, be disciplined. This could lead her to become irresponsible since she perceives you won't be "tough" with her. The end result could be that her performance deteriorates.

But the boomerang loop with undesirable and unintended consequences isn't over yet. Your employee's reaction could cause you to conclude your efforts were wrong. To counteract the problem, you may begin being so tough on her that she, confused by your actions, concludes you're unpredictable and mercurial.

Always look at the whole process, all the relevant variables and how they interrelate to each other.

Are There Left-Brained and Right-Brained People?
I'm sure most have heard of the theory of "left-brain" and "right-brain" thinking, where the left side of our brain allegedly controls a logical and analytical thought process and the right side controls our more creative endeavors.

Though the body's different operating thoughts and actions do originate with specific areas of the brain, some scientists question whether an individual can accurately be stereotyped as either a "left brain" or "right brain" person. The common thinking used to be that those who were good at math were "left-brain" people, but recent research reveals when we do anything mathematical, we're drawing from both sides of our brains, not just the left side.

A simple label rarely defines a person's entire personality, which is something you need to remember when dealing with your employees. Try not to pigeon-hole anyone by generalizing who they might be as people.

What is important for you to remember is your employees, like everyone, are both logical and creative, given the right circumstances. Some may appear to be more analytical than the majority of your other workers, while a few may be highly creative. But change the situation slightly and you may be surprised to find your very logical person suddenly becoming more creative.

Although some may have a dominant inclination to logical or creative thinking, it's probably more reasonable to use the theory as a way to differentiate between types of behavior, rather than to generalize a dominant pattern in a person.

What is clear is you and your workers will be called upon to use all your personal resources—your emotional, creative, logical and analytical thinking—when you set up your systems.

Balance is the key.

Set Up a System

Many leaders erroneously make one of two assumptions when they tell their employees to do something. They either believe: 1) that simple instruction is sufficient, or 2) they need to follow up constantly to make sure their employees are following instructions.

Both of these can have disastrous impacts.

In most cases, if you assume you can speak it once and that's all

Work Leader's Tip: Use Systems Responsibly

When used properly, the following systems are time-saving tools which can help you and your workers:

- A regularly-scheduled routine management meeting with your staff where the most critical priorities are discussed and you can see how everyone's progressing toward the goal.
- "Management By Wandering Around" (MBWA), where you wander around your unit, randomly checking on everyone's progress and informally discussing the project with them.
- Customer Relationship Management (CRM) software and apps to track down new leads, check client or project status and follow-up on requirements.
- Electronic calendars and contact or address book software and apps which you can sync to your computer, tablet and smartphone.

that's necessary, you're setting yourself up for failure. You do occasionally need to make sure everyone's on track.

But you're going to have problems, too, if you feel you have to constantly do follow-ups. A capable staff will resent your excessive control or micromanaging. They'll believe you don't trust them and will begin "allowing" you to manage their duties, since they assume you've taken over their bottom-line responsibility for the work.

The best solution is to have the systems in place to assure you know what the current state of your unit's performance is—without having to micromanage or ignore your employees until the job's completed.

Enter Peter Drucker

Management consultant Peter Drucker was one of the most prolific writers on organizational leadership during the twentieth century. He's often referred to as the father of modern management and was one of the first to define several critical functions referred to as the mechanics of management, including: planning, organizing, directing and controlling.

You're only going to be able to effectively execute your plan if you have people and systems in place to generate superior results. You have to establish expectations, but simply establishing goals without plans is fruitless. Plans are the pathways which define how you'll achieve the results.

Many writers on leadership make a distinction between leading and managing, implying management is a lower skill—a position with no merit—but I don't see it that way. Those "in charge" are required to lead and manage. Leading is what you do for and with people. Managing is what you do to make sure you and your unit achieve those goals. They work together.

Remember from earlier chapters, "assignment" requires you to assign the right people to to the right jobs. After you do that, you have to "organize" and "direct" your workers with structure, effective work processes and systems to support your plan's execution. In addition, you need to find a way to assure the processes are executed properly. That's one of your critical roles.

With "direction" in place, you and your staff have to have the "controls" to make sure systems are in place to monitor progress and make any mid-course corrections. You should be able to delegate many aspects of the plan's execution, but delegation without control is abrogation.

So let's take a closer look at planning, organizing, directing and controlling

Planning

Setting expectations is the first step in a plan, but, in order to make a difference, you have to be specific and detailed.

That means you need to find a way to measure your employees' accountability, first with their assignment of responsibility and then with a specified time for them to complete their tasks. Your plan has to adequately detail the action steps, resources required, assigned responsibility and deadlines to be met.

If you establish a vague plan, you'll probably have a vague result. Be specific. We covered that in the chapter on expectations.

Timing for completion is a critical element. Plans have to be executed in a timely manner or they become accidents.

Plans also have to be documented, meaning they have to be written. Yes, it's necessary for you to write it down. There's no better test of clarity in thinking than forcing your thoughts onto paper. Vague ideas about your plans will only succeed in making your workers unsure and confused. Write it down.

Organization

An essential part of executing your plan is to assign and organize your staff, along with the necessary resources, in order to achieve peak performance.

You can organize in an informal manner, such as verbally stating your general guidelines, telling your workers who does what job and how it's to be done. Or you can create very detailed and structured flow charts, defining each step in the process and showing who reports to whom.

Many companies use a pyramid, "one boss," "top down," hierarchical authority structure based on the way the military is organized. That's pretty simple and straightforward.

But as companies grow larger and more complex, some are now opting for shared responsibility through a "matrix" organization. For

---

Work Leader's **Tip:** Are Systems Working for You?

Do you have systems in place in your routine? Or do you operate in random chaos each day? To find out, ask yourself if you:

- Have a drawer full of business cards which have never been entered into a formal contact file.
- Spend unnecessary time looking for phone numbers or contact information you know you should have saved.
- Wish you were more organized.
- Have trouble accomplishing both professional and personal tasks on a given day.
- Forget to follow through on something because the reminder note got lost in the papers on your desk.
- Forget to review and update your checklist at the end of the day so you know what you need to do tomorrow.
- Feel there's never enough time in the day.
- Spend every weekend doing personal chores you couldn't fit in during the week.

---

instance, a group of people who normally work for different bosses in a company may come together for a specific project, which has a new boss. That makes the workers responsible not only to their regular managers, but also the special project's manager. The sharing of responsibilities works more efficiently with larger organizations where there's a need to coordinate across many different "top down" pyramids.

Whichever system you choose to use, remember your key to success is clarity. The members of your organization have to have a clear understanding of their responsibilities and assignments. Any ambiguity regarding these factors will cause confusion and, ultimately, failure to achieve the unit's goals.

Directing

Never assume only issuing instructions to your workers once at the beginning of a project is enough to complete the goal. Simply assigning tasks and walking away is a good way to fail, with your workers putting in an inadequate performance.

You need to be actively directing them, not like an overprotective mother hen, but enough to be apprised of the current progress of your unit's project. Always touch base with your employees throughout the process.

With a traditional model, you tell your staff what to do and then you continue to check in on them. Or, you can delegate that responsibility to one of your workers.

Some managers believe self-directed teams are more effective than "one boss" models. With that, your staff assumes the responsibility to direct their own activities and report the team's progress. That only works if your team members are sufficiently motivated and disciplined to self-direct themselves. But if your group doesn't come together, or if workers aren't committed to achieving results, you won't get effective progress.

Consider how well disciplined your employees are, then choose the best model for them and you. Whatever direction you decide to take, just make sure there's some way you can track your staff's ability to stay focused on the results.

Controlling

You can plan, organize and direct effectively and still fail. If your organization's going to achieve the desired results, you have to have a system of controls in place to keep your staff on track in the event they start to veer off course. Even the most automated process requires a mechanism to assure the mechanical processes stay in control.

When management consultants W. Edwards Deming and Joseph Juran convinced Japanese businesses they'd have better success if they instituted statistical controls on their manufacturing processes, it changed the course of Japanese (and U.S.) history. Those controls, which alerted managers and workers when production was out of "control limits," helped companies make appropriate adjustments in order to assure their output would be within the appropriate tolerances.

You and your organization have to have process controls in place, too. They can be as simple as a daily report of the quantity of outputs your unit's completed or as complex as a detailed "dashboard" which measures everything influencing the results.

Whatever the mechanism, you have to know how your unit's performing—and soon enough to make "mid-course" adjustments. Waiting until the end of the time required to complete a project or achieve a goal is unacceptable. There have to be intermediate measures available so you know how your employees are progressing.

Without these control checkpoints along the way, the chance of your unit achieving of success is slim.

Summary
Systems provide the structure which allows you to lead a more efficient and productive life. Complicated or complex technology isn't required to create an effective system of managing your calendar, your contact file and your task list. Systems are simply a method of organization which save time and aid productivity.

In this era of information overload, you can't rely on your memories or sticky notes as sufficient reminders to follow through on your tasks.

Benjamin Franklin, one of America's founding fathers, struggled with time management and order. To combat the problem, he devised a plan: each day he'd create a schedule listing his goals and tasks, assigned in hourly segments. Each evening he'd review the day's activities and accomplishments, asking, "What good have I done today?"

"This emphasis on setting goals for the day ahead and taking stock afterward remains a staple of time-management advice. (At least, so I'm told.)," writes Justin Fox, a *Fortune* magazine editor-at-large, in a March 2006 article titled "What Ben Franklin Can Teach Execs."[28]

Fox writes he's far more likely to accomplish something when he has a well-defined to-do list for the day, as do most of us. But, he adds, "...in a work world where conflicting, competing priorities are the norm, it's really hard to stick to such a list. Which is why most of us seldom get around to devising one."

Even with his extensive to-do list, Franklin wrote that he still found "emergency fires" which kept cropping up throughout his day, throwing his well-written schedule completely out of whack.

He wrote in his autobiography, "I never arrived at the perfection

I had been so ambitious of attaining, but fell far short of it, yet I was, by the endeavor, a better and happier man."[29]

Franklin failed at staying 100 percent on track with his schedule and you will, too. The good news is, even though he didn't finish everything on his daily lists, Benjamin Franklin did accomplish a lot, as you will. Whether or not you succeed in checking off each task on your daily list, you'll be more productive and focused simply by having a list.

That may seem elementary, but it's a system which will help you set goals and determine which assignments are necessary to achieve them. Each assignment should be given a deadline which is reasonable, but still ambitious. A sense of urgency is better than feeling you have plenty of time to "slack off." At the end of the day, you'll have a great sense of satisfaction at how much you were able to accomplish and be better able to assess what you need to do tomorrow.

Professional and personal "to-do" lists are critical for us to accomplish our assignments and goals. Whether you need to remind yourself to follow up on a list of client prospects or pick up the dry cleaning and groceries after work, you need to schedule those activities in your daily plans.

In theory, it's best to keep your professional and personal lists separate, but you do need to know your twenty-four-hour availability when scheduling appointments, so it may be to your advantage to combine them.

There's no need to spend a fortune on day planners since many calendars, contact organizers and to-do lists are available online and in electronic form on computers, smartphones and tablets.

Systems are intended to make your work run more smoothly and efficiently, with less effort and less chance of error. They enable you to connect with your staff, energize them, focus them and lead them. Just make sure you have systems in place and a way of monitoring your unit's progress as they move toward their goals.

They need to be constantly checked against actual work achievement, as well as updated and maintained to assure they're relevant and current, the same way you update your calendar or client database.

Case Study

Brent was recruited to join a fast-growing website development company which provides the whole gamut of services, from designing and building new sites to hosting the sites and optimizing them for search engines.

Although the company's based in a medium-sized community, it's quickly expanded from servicing local clients to landing some large national accounts. Brent's role as account director means he interacts with clients and also manages the programmers, technicians and design - ers who make up the young, creative development team.

Before accepting the job, Brent reviewed many of the websites the company had created and was convinced he'd be leading a team of high - ly talented individuals. But after just a short time on the job, it became apparent he'd joined a company in total chaos.

For reasons unbeknownst to him, a succession of account managers had left the company in the last several months. The turnover was creat - ing disorder, confusion and a lack of accountability. Despite a talented team which put in long hours at work, everyone was far behind on their deadlines. Clients were complaining about the delays and lack of response from the individuals assigned to their website projects.

The failed deadlines led Brent's boss, Jerome, to put increased pressure on his associates. Rather than acting as a motivating force, Jerome expressed anger and dissatisfaction, which had a negative impact on morale. The work environment reminded Brent of a boiling hot kitchen full of frenzied cooks, none of whom was telling the others what he was adding to the pot on the stove. No one knew what he was supposed to cook.

Rather than quit like the many account managers before him, Brent decided to save his job, as well as help his team live up to its potential and achieve success.

He analyzed the situation and determined his team would be capa - ble of great work if they were simply given a system which would allow everyone to keep track of project assignments, milestones and deadlines.

Brent set a meeting with Jerome and presented his suggestion for the company to invest in Customer Relationship Management (CRM) soft - ware would allow him to assign individual workers to each task within a project, control the flow of assignments as each task was completed and establish deadlines which would be known to everyone involved. With projects so tightly and transparently organized, there would be no confu - sion as to whether a task had been completed and who was responsible for it.

Jerome liked Brent's idea and commended him for researching the various software options, as well as recommending one which was mid-range in price, but had all the capabilities they'd need to manage projects.

After some discussion, they decided to hire a receptionist who would be responsible for fielding calls and requests from clients and entering those assignments into the system. To prevent the complaint that associ - ates were unresponsive, they'd be instructed to forward email requests from clients to the new receptionist, who would also input those assign - ments into the system. Employees were further instructed to stay focused by handling their individual tasks according to their order in the queue, rather than trying to handle each new task immediately as it came in, leaving others unfinished.

Two months after implementing the new CRM system, Jerome called Brent into his office.

"Brent, I can't understand what you've done wrong as a manager, but we lost two big clients this week. That's on top of the one we lost last week and they'd been with us since we started the business. As the account director, you're responsible for interacting with clients. You should have known they were unhappy and done something to fix it. We can't afford to lose these clients and unless you can convince me your team will improve immediately, I don't need to waste any more money on you."

The client dissatisfaction shocked Brent. He understood why his boss Jerome was upset, but he didn't feel he was the sole employee responsible for keeping clients happy and on board. Rather than argue, he decided to get to the bottom of what went wrong.

"Did the clients explain why they were upset enough to cancel their engagements with us?" Brent asked.

"Yes, and it was the same in every case," said Jerome. "They said their requests and problems weren't addressed in a timely manner. Their calls and emails weren't returned, communication was essentially nonexistent and deadlines weren't met."

Brent was still dumfounded.

"The CRM system should have prevented all of this," he said. "I can't understand what happened because the team's working really long hours."

He promised to call a meeting of every associate on the development team and get to the bottom of the problem. This was his only hope to solve the problem and save his job.

So what went wrong and who was to blame?

The problem was there was no human oversight. The system was left to function on its own without human thought. No one had thought to indicate priority calls.

The new receptionist hadn't been told existing clients needed imme - diate attention, so she'd listed their calls in the order they came in, behind all the new callers, instead of being assigned a higher priority in the queue. They were far down the list, so it took a while before anyone on the team got to them.

Not only was the receptionist not putting urgent clients at the top of the list, but employees were using the system blindly, instead of scanning the list of callers to spot a client whose website was malfunctioning and needed immediate communication and attention.

Everyone in the organization was relying on the system to make rational decisions when systems actually work the opposite way: humans have to input information based on rational thought in order for the sys - tems to function as intended.

So who's to blame?

First, Brent's boss didn't exhibit positive leadership behavior by addressing his staff with anger and abrasive language and he's partly to blame for the situation. He never bothered to check how the new system was working.

Brent's team also shares responsibility for losing the clients because they weren't communicating with them and meeting deadlines.

But the bottom line is Brent's responsible for whether his team is achieving success. The blame for their failure ultimately rests on his shoulders.

Brent should have been monitoring the assignments and their status. He also should have been personally communicating with the clients, a defined part of his job. If he'd communicated with them, he would have known they were unhappy. If he'd monitored the status of the assignments in the CRM system, he would have known deadlines weren't being met.

His belief that he isn't the only person responsible for the clients' hap - piness suggests he doesn't really understand he's failed as a leader to sup - port his team and give them the human tools (not just automated tools) which are required for success.

chapter eight

HUMOR
Lighten Up and Ditch Hubris for Humility

If you want want the best performance from your associates, you have to incorporate humor into your workplace. It's the best way to promote teamwork, creativity and job satisfaction.

Unfortunately, it's a fundamental joy which is absent from many jobs.

As a leader, it's important for you to laugh and lighten the mood each day and encourage your associates to do the same. That's because most employees would prefer to work at places which embrace humor, rather than organizations which are somber and depressing.

True, your workers have to be diligent and disciplined with what they're doing, but they need a counterbalance to help them alleviate the daily stress which comes with most jobs. The extremely competitive work environment which dominates our society increases employees' stress, as does the need to constantly learn new things in order to advance and, in this age of high unemployment, their ever present fear of losing their jobs.

If you ease your workers' levels of stress, you'll help promote their well-being, but if you don't and their stress continues without any kind of relief, it can lead to health problems ranging from headaches, nausea, high blood pressure and sleep disturbances to chest pain and even death.

Even if people are strong enough to avoid the more serious health problems resulting from stress, it still can negatively impact their immune system, making them more prone to illness. In fact, research shows stress can cause or worsen diseases, such as cancer, as well as emotional problems, which can result in accidents, depression and suicide.

As a leader, you need to make it a priority to reduce your workers' stress—and the best way is with humor.

The Benefits of Humor

Just as stress negatively impacts your health, humor impacts it in a positive way.

The Mayo Clinic says laughter is a great way to get relief from stress because it stimulates a person's muscles, lungs and heart, as well as increases the feel-good endorphins which the brain releases.

Studies have shown physiologically that laughter produces the same benefits as mild exercise: we breathe more rapidly, which gets more oxygen into our system, and our heart rate gets a boost. Some studies show humor may even increase our infection-fighting antibodies.

Humor can create such a positive atmosphere in the workplace that your employees will find it easier to have more positive attitudes. That, in turn, will defuse anger and result in less absenteeism, even lower employee turnover, while inspiring more creativity.

The current generation of employees expects to work longer hours than were typical for previous generations, but they're also looking for a fun, supportive environment which is more relaxed than the formal, buttoned-up office culture of the past.

"If your employees are happy and have a full, fun-filled, balanced life, they will bring greater energy and enthusiasm to the workplace and your department, agency or company will function at peak performance," wrote Ann Fry, a humor coach from Austin, Texas, in her book *Laughing Matters: The Value of Humor in the Workplace*. Fry offers a simple formula for a better workplace environment, "...a willingness to laugh + a sense of lightheartedness = a fun and productive workplace."[30]

Humor isn't rocket science, but without it, you may end up with unhappy employees who are looking elsewhere for a job—and employee turnover is expensive for an organization. It takes time and money to interview, train and integrate each new employee.

Studies have also shown organizations which allow a little fun at work are extraordinarily successful.

"Have fun," said Andrew Bridge, the managing director of Virgin

Mobile Canada, part of Sir Richard Bransen's Virgin Group Inc. Bridge wrote in a November 16, 2012 article which appeared in the *Globe and Mail*, "It may seem simple, but a fun workplace is a happy workplace."[31]

Virgin Global isn't the only successful corporation which feels that way. So do giants such as: Southwest Airlines, Chevron, Google, HBO, Disney and ESPN.

"I think people should have fun at work," said Herb Kelleher, co-founder of Southwest Airlines, in a CNBC interview. "It should be an enjoyable part of their life. They should gain psychic satisfaction from it. I think most of us enjoy fun, and why not at work, as well as at play? And so we've always encouraged people to be themselves, not to be robotic, not to be automatons. We don't expect you to surrender your natural personality when you join Southwest Airlines. We want you to have some fun."[32]

Southwest's fun translates into a positive effect on the bottom-line results, too. The airline:

- Has the fewest customer complaints more than twenty-five years in a row, according to the Department of Transportation Air Travel Consumer Report
- Has been profitable for thirty-nine consecutive years
- Is consistently named one of *Fortune* magazine's top ten most admired companies
- Boasts a less-than-five-percent employee turnover rate.

Why Don't Leaders Use More Humor?

If Southwest and other big-name organizations are using humor and succeeding, why are so many leaders reluctant to do the same?

The first reason is perception: they mistakenly believe humor and laughter in the workplace means associates aren't doing their jobs. They may also feel it's inappropriate and unprofessional. The second reason is personal. Many leaders don't consider themselves funny, don't understand the value of humor and don't know how to incorporate fun into work.

The first reason is simply a misconception. Humor doesn't undermine work. To the contrary, it enhances an associate's ability to perform. Humor provides a physical and emotional release, a distraction from negative emotions, such as anger or stress, and it enables us to see challenges from a different perspective.

Laughter is contagious: it elevates the mood of those around us and creates a positive social interaction. Whether one associate is having a bad day or a team of associates is facing a difficult situation at work, laughter will temporarily divert attention away from the problem and will likely improve their ability to cope with the challenge.

"For too many companies, building a team means creating a high-powered, smoothly functioning organization that has plenty of muscle, but not much heart. It is the absence of the human side of business that depletes employee morale, and contributes to job dissatisfaction and burnout," writes Matt Weinstein in his book *Managing to Have Fun: How Fun at Work Can: Motivate Your Employees, Inspire Your Coworkers, Boost Your Bottom Line.*[33]

Weinstein founded the company Playfair, a management consulting company which provides team-building to other corporations.

"By adding an element of fun and celebration to a team-building program," continues Weinstein, "you can take an important step toward humanizing your workplace and creating a sense of heart and soul in your organization."

Humor in the workplace does involve some risk. You want to incorporate humor and lighten the tone of the work environment, but not let it get out of control. That can result in your employees reducing their focus and productivity. You also want to make sure the fun doesn't become offensive to employees in any way. Brutal practical jokes, off-color comments or politically incorrect statements and behavior don't belong in the workplace.

Keep it clean, but lighten up just a little.

Humor Displays Humility

Show you care about your employees' health and happiness by lightening up and easing their stress with humor. Leading with humility and humor is the only option, but, remember, attitude is the key.

When you lead with humility you show your associates you truly love them and consider yourself one of them. On the other hand, if you exhibit hubris and take yourself too seriously, they'll not only think you consider yourself superior to them, but that you're stern and unsympathetic. That kind of attitude isn't likely to win their loyalty and trust and will probably result in unhappy and stressed out people.

Humor in the workplace can be as simple as keeping a smile on your face or cheering up an employee with a kind act and supportive words.

"My definition of healthy workplace humor is 'acts involving some sort of surprise and/or exaggeration that make people feel good,' writes psychotherapist and stand-up comic David Granirer on his website. "Certainly this can take the form of joke telling, but it can also take many others. Leaving a cookie on a coworker's desk, giving an unexpected compliment, and sending an encouraging e-mail are all acts that involve some form of surprise ('Hey, I wasn't expecting that!') and leave people feeling good."[34]

Granirer, who provides motivational and team-building seminars on laughter in the workplace, writes, "...healthy workplace humor accomplishes four main goals: It releases tension, creates a sense of acceptance, conveys a sense of unity or support, and restores a healthy perspective on a given situation."

Adding humor requires you make a conscious effort to develop a culture of fun in your workplace. There are countless ways to lighten the mood or cause a laugh and you don't have to be a funny person to incorporate this element into your leadership role.

Don't try to be a comedian if it's not your style and don't cross the line of what's appropriate in a professional environment. Your office isn't a comedy club. It's a place where your associates should feel it's fun to work. In many respects, using humor simply shows you're supportive, nurturing and caring.

The impact humor has on you is equally important. You need to release stress or you won't be able to make rational decisions, be receptive to your associates or achieve your goals. Your health and well-being are just as important as that of your employees.

How to Incorporate Humor in the Workplace

There's no formula for incorporating humor into your business. You, your organization and the individuals who work there are unique.

The first step is to make a personal assessment of your own humor quotient. Ask friends and family to give you an honest assessment of your "fun factor." How and when do you most readily exhibit your humor? Use their feedback to determine ways in which you'll feel at ease expressing your sense of fun and lightheartedness.

If you're truly "humor-impaired," seek a mentor to help uncover your sense of humor.

Look for humor in everyday situations, as well as in reading material and interactions with others. Compile a humor library of jokes, quotes, cartoons, bumper stickers, articles and stories which make you laugh. In moments of stress, take time to read one of the items again and share it with your staff. The result of your humor won't only be a pleasure for your associates, but it'll also help you release tension and maintain a positive attitude.

The next step is to assess your employees' personalities and the level of humor they currently display in the workplace. Consider what type of humor will be well-received within the organization. Wearing a clown nose to a staff meeting might not garner laughs, but breaking the ice by telling a joke on yourself could set the group at ease. Gentle, self-deprecating humor is a way to demonstrate to others you're human. By showing you don't take yourself too seriously, others will feel more relaxed and comfortable expressing themselves in your presence.

Establishing your own precedent for humor is essential because you have to lead by example. You can't expect your associates to embrace humor if you don't exhibit that behavior yourself. Your attitude will affect your associates and their attitudes are likely to mirror your own. A funny, quick-witted associate will quickly learn to save his jokes for after hours if you frown or fail to laugh along with the others. A shy, quiet associate is likely to lighten up and become more spirited if you display a sense of humor and participate in the fun. Fun doesn't function if it's not shared. This means your personal commitment to the benefits of humor, and your own pleasure in sharing it, has to be genuine.

If you connect with your associates on a human level (and love them), you'll instinctively want to celebrate their successes, share kind words and alleviate tension. You'll enjoy your role as a leader and it'll be evident in your attitude. As a result, you'll elicit great attitudes and loyalty from your associates. If you feel isolated and lonely at the top, then your abilities as a leader will be severely compromised. The fun factor isn't just for your team's benefit—it's for you, too.

The attitudes and environment in your organization can't be

changed in a day. It takes time and should be approached in increments. Consider your typical routine as well as your staff's. In what ways can you introduce a surprise to break up the routine and make it a more pleasant place to work for everyone involved? If you have a weekly staff meeting in the conference room, consider holding it in a different place, such as a local restaurant. When the weather's nice, meet outside.

Bring bagels to a morning meeting or choose a different associate each week to have a surprise snack delivered for the team. If the group has to work especially late one evening to meet a deadline, send them all home with gift certificates for pizza delivery as a way to show your appreciation.

Demonstrating your appreciation can take many forms, and the more creative you are, the more fun it'll be. At Playfair, Matt Weinstein likes to express his thanks by having flowers delivered anonymously to an associate. The accompanying note tells the recipient he or she is appreciated and, within a half-hour, they should pass along the flowers to another coworker to show their own appreciation for someone else. Such gestures aren't expensive or grandiose, but they do promote positive feelings and attitudes.

Convincing the Boss About Humor's Benefits

What happens if your own boss doesn't readily embrace the concept of humor in the workplace because he or she is set in the belief work is "serious" business which doesn't include laughter and fun?

You don't want to lose your job, but you also don't want to fail employees in your unit by ignoring humor. A good start would be to have an honest conversation with your supervisor and tell him or her you've been reading literature to help you improve as a leader. Explain how experts and case studies have convinced you humor leads to greater productivity and job satisfaction. Give examples of the ways in which levity helps people feel and perform better. Your boss will probably need time to digest your information, but, hopefully, your example will lead to a change in attitude at the top of your organization.

As you and your staff become more comfortable with humor, you should share the responsibility of bringing humor into the workplace. Appoint a humor ambassador or ask everyone to make suggestions for ways fun and levity can be incorporated into your workplace. If you make having fun at work a priority, you'll discover countless ways to act on it, as well as countless rewards for your efforts.

"Laughter and play on the job are not an end in and of themselves. They are a doorway, an entrée into being more human with the people we work with," writes Matt Weinstein in his book *Managing to Have Fun*. "The only way to keep a sense of fun and play in your work life is to consciously choose to make it a priority."[35]

One of the greatest benefits of humor is it puts people at ease, which promotes creative thinking.

"If necessity is the mother of invention, play is the father," wrote Roger von Oech in his book *A Whack on the Side of the Head: How You Can Be More Creative*. "It is when you are not taking yourself seriously that your defenses are down, your mental locks are loosened, and there is little concern with the rules, or being wrong."[36]

News ideas most often arise from creative rather than analytical thinking. When you create an accepting, fun atmosphere which welcomes "crazy" notions, you may be surprised how brilliant those ideas turn out to be. Brainstorming sessions will be more productive when humor is involved because they break down the barriers of self-consciousness. If there's no "right" answer, every thought or contribution is valid and welcome.

Some leaders use jokes or props to lighten the mood and promote laughter, while others use games or gags. It doesn't matter which methods you use to bring humor to the table, just enjoy the fun together as a team. Laughter creates an energy and camaraderie which bridges gaps. You and your employees will be more comfortable with each other, more receptive to each other's thoughts and more willing to share your "crazy" ideas.

Promoting Creative Thinking

One strategy for prompting creative thinking is to play the "yes and..." game. It starts with one person tossing out an idea which can be practical or zany. The next person says "yes and...," then adds something to it and each member of the group joins in.

For example, a leader might gather his creative team together to discuss ways to increase public awareness of the company. The first idea might be "You should host an event," while the next person might say, "Yes, and it should have a memorable theme." The next might say, "Yes, and there should be a contest."

By having only "yes" replies, there's no fear of being wrong and you keep the the spirit and nature of the session based on fun. Even if the ideas become impractical as the chain of yeses continues, there will likely be a few suggestions or kernels of creativity which may ultimately lead to an "aha."

For associates to be able to participate in this sort of freestyle thinking and sharing, they have to be open to humor. Everyone knows how to laugh, but there are some individuals who will find it challenging to lighten up and enjoy levity in the workplace. They may have the same fears leaders have: that they won't be taken seriously or will appear unprofessional. It's your responsibility to establish the humor precedent and help your employees join in the fun. It's an aspect of associate development which is important for long-term success. Associates who can't learn to lighten up and maintain a healthy attitude may run the risk of burning out or leaving the organization altogether.

Are Your Job Candidates Open to Humor?

In establishing a workplace which embraces humor, you also need to consider whether potential hires are a good fit in your environment. The tone of a job interview is typically serious, causing candidates to most likely behave in a strictly professional manner. This presents a problem for you when you're trying to gauge a candidate's humor quotient.

To the extent it's possible, try to put the candidate at ease and take note of whether they smile often. If appropriate, tell a joke or humorous personal story and see if it elicits a laugh. When it's too hard to assess whether a candidate can lighten up, address the issue openly. Explain your team takes work seriously, but laughter and fun are part of the culture. Ask the candidate if that's an environment where he or she would be comfortable. Use the clues from body language, attitude and dialogue to determine if an individual will mesh with your team and be able to participate in the fun.

Humor Diffuses Workplace Stress

When faced with difficult circumstances, your ability to use humor to diffuse stress and tension will actually help your associates regain their focus and enthusiasm.

A loving boss recognizes an associate's happiness and productivity involves more than what goes on at work. Most employees will try to organize their personal and professional lives so they run smoothly and don't negatively affect one another, but, inevitably, there will be times when their family will take precedence and interfere with their work. There are also times when work demands they sacrifice or put on hold certain aspects of their personal lives.

When a valued and reliable employee is simply having a bad day, respond in a sensitive way. Rather than a reprimand which will make the person feel worse, ease the tension through humor. Tell your associate to take a breather of some sort. If one associate is having a bad day, the negative attitude could affect other associates and lower their morale. It could also become evident to customers or clients. By helping the individual in distress, you also help the people who would be interacting with him or her.

Start with Your Comfort Zone

If you don't consider yourself funny or good at telling jokes, focus on your sense of humor and what makes you laugh. Start with your comfort zone and then expand on it. Make it a personal challenge to seek out humor and come up with creative ways to share it with your associates. Remember, humor isn't just "funny," but also includes unexpected gestures which are encouraging and kind.

The following is a list of ways you can begin to incorporate humor into your daily life and work:

- Set the example for your staff: smile, laugh, be upbeat and friendly.
- Take every opportunity to find humor in day-to-day events.
- Tell a joke on yourself.
- Find humor both in travail and success.

- Break the ice with a funny anecdote.
- Hold brainstorming sessions in which funny, wacky and crazy ideas are encouraged.
- Arrange an office contest for something silly such as the best self-portrait done with finger paint.
- Ask your associates for anonymous suggestions on ways to incorporate fun into their work, then select some and put them into practice.
- Designate a humor ambassador.
- Establish a casual attire day.
- Organize one fun outing each month.
- Create a welcoming ritual for new employees.
- Play "yes and..." to promote creative ideas.
- Recognize when stress levels have reached a high and call a time-out.
- Take your staff to lunch.
- Order in a pizza.
- Send everyone outside for some fresh air.
- Hold staff meetings in a variety of locations.
- Break up the routine with a surprise.
- Take the staff to see a comedy film.
- Give each associate a joke-a-day calendar.
- Subscribe to an online humor newsletter.
- Incorporate elements of surprise, exaggeration and fun. Think of ways to surprise your staff and encourage them to enjoy the moment.
- Seek out humor in your own life so you feel comfortable when it's time to lighten up and elicit a laugh.
- Attend a comedy club show.
- Read the strange (but true) news at www.news.aol.com/strange.
- Play with kids. They're sure to make you laugh.
- Visit a toy store.
- Practice random acts of kindness.
- Have the staff spend a day doing charitable work because it promotes good feelings.
- Pay the toll for the car behind you and watch the driver's expressions of confusion and delight.

- Buy popcorn for the person in line next to you.
- Build a collection of funny cartoons, articles, bumper stickers, jokes, photos and stories and share it with others.
- Give a surprise gift of recognition which has to be passed on.
- Send humorous cards to associates on special occasions.
- Celebrate the holidays with themed decorations and parties.
- Organize a staff retreat at an amusement park.
- Post a bulletin board with jokes, quotes and cartoons.
- Create a humor zone at work and fill it with toys and games.
- Use silly props which are so absurd they overcome everyone's programming to behave like adults.
- Have a witty backup plan for when jokes fall flat.
- Take an improv class.
- The next time you laugh, make it so loud everyone around you can hear it.

It Helps to be Happy

Do you want to feel angry and stressed out, or do you want to feel positive and upbeat?

The principle of humor should be an easy one to embrace, since most people want to be happy. Humor's most significant factor toward helping you be a good leader is it affects the physical and mental health of both you and your employees. Your health impacts every aspect of your life, including your ability to enjoy your family, friends, hobbies and activities outside of work. Humor is one of the most important areas where you can really nurture yourself.

Humor as it applies to you as a Work Leader isn't always about laughter or even "lightening up." Besides being in tune with your employees and helping them make the necessary changes which will help them better cope with the stress in their lives, it's about recognizing you may have to make some changes in your own life for the very same reason.

When one of my co-workers took on a lot of personal commitments, she had less free time for her own activities during the evening. The problem, as she readily admits, is she isn't a "morning person." Although she doesn't show up late, she isn't one who would voluntarily suggest an early morning breakfast meeting. She prefers to have time before work to go through her morning routine without feeling rushed. Her routine includes reading the newspaper cover to cover, which is actually essential to her job and something she chooses to do before going to the office. She's also athletic and enjoys being physically active for the stress release as well as the health benefits.

When family obligations and her involvement with a local charity increased the demands on her time after work, she ended up with no time left in the evening for exercise. That had a negative impact on her happiness and caused her to feel stressed and disappointed in herself, as well as unhappy she was missing out on something which gave her pleasure.

A few months into her new, busier schedule, she realized she had to find a way to incorporate exercise back into her routine because it was an essential activity for her well-being. Now, her alarm rings an hour earlier and she goes straight to the gym for a fifty-minute workout. Despite having to wake up early, she says her attitude and outlook have improved tremendously because she starts the day by accomplishing something which makes her feel happy and good about herself. Furthermore, she says she's much more upbeat and relaxed at work when she's satisfied and that's essential for her on a personal level.

As a leader, you have to find ways to embrace happiness and humor in order to cope with stress in your own life. Make an honest assessment of your own personal needs and the things which make you happy. What are your hobbies? Do you enjoy playing sports, cooking, reading, watching movies, working for a charity or simply spending time with friends and family? Whatever it is that makes you feel good and helps recharge your batteries should be given a priority in your daily routine.

Sometimes circumstances change and there no longer seems to be a convenient time to fit your personal stress-relieving activities into the day. That's when you need to take a step back and reorganize your schedule. Most people feel so many demands on their time, they end up sacrificing what they want to do for what they have to do. In the long-term this is unhealthy because it ignores the role humor plays in your life. If something which provides personal happiness and pleasure is made a priority, there's always a way to find time for it.

It's essential for you to identify a couple of personal priorities for yourself and then schedule them in your routine. When "self" priorities are set as appointments in your calendar, they're less likely to be ignored or delayed for when you "have time." You may need to adjust other activities in your schedule to accommodate your personal priorities, but, in the long run, you'll be a happier, healthier person who functions better at work, as well as at home.

The basis of humor is treating yourself as someone who requires understanding and nurturing.

Case Study—Anne's Bad Day

Anne works as a senior reporter for a local newspaper in a large city. The reporters and editors usually meet first thing in the morning to discuss the latest local developments, brainstorm on story ideas and receive their daily reporting assignments.

One morning the meeting was scheduled for earlier than usual. There was more to discuss due to the upcoming elections and a recent storm which had caused a lot of local damage. As a features writer for human interest stories, Anne was responsible for interviewing some storm victims who had suffered damage to their homes and power outages at their businesses.

When she was about to leave for work, her twelve-year-old son David announced he was sick and planning to stay home from school. After talking to him, she realized he wasn't ill, but merely trying to get out of taking a math test. After forty-five minutes of cajoling and threatening him, she finally got him to get dressed and get in the car. Now she was late.

After she'd dropped off David at school, Anne headed to the office, but because she'd gotten such a late start, she was stuck in the worst of rush hour traffic. She arrived at the newsroom well after the morning meeting had concluded.

Because she was a highly regarded reporter and conscientious employee, it was upsetting for her to have personal issues affecting her professional life. Furthermore, she knew she'd have several new assignments for the day and would be under even more pressure to meet her deadlines. She went directly to Jim, the managing editor, to apologize and find out what she'd missed in the meeting.

Jim was very understanding since he'd worked with Anne for several years and knew she wouldn't have been late without a legitimate reason. He reassured her he was sympathetic and had faced similar challenges with his own children. After discussing her assignments, Anne went back to her desk. She began making calls for interviews and checking facts on the two stories assigned to her. The newsroom was a large, open space, so Jim was able to see and hear what happened next.

When Anne began checking the facts an intern had researched for her story, she noticed several errors and inconsistencies. Frustrated because she knew the mistakes meant she'd have to redo the research herself, some - thing which would take more time than she had, she called the intern to her desk and immediately began verbally ripping into him, humiliating the young man in front of the whole newsroom.

Ten minutes later, a woman Anne had planned to profile for a storm-related human interest piece called to say she didn't want the public attention and backed out of the interview. Anne was frantic, knowing she'd have to start from scratch on both stories. That meant she was going to have to stay late to finish writing them.

She thought of her son coming home from school to an empty house and started feeling as though she'd break down in tears if her day contin - ued like this. She simply couldn't handle the weight of her responsibili - ties and the pressure. Her head began to pound and she found it difficult to focus on what to do next.

From across the room, Jim observed Anne deteriorating under the stress. He knew she was strong and capable, but he was afraid if her mood didn't improve, she'd continue lashing out at others just as she'd done to the intern. Since he was understaffed and couldn't afford to send her home until she'd completed her assigned stories, he tried to think of something which would improve the situation.

What can Jim do to diffuse the tension?

This is a perfect example of a time when humor and the human touch can be especially effective. Anne was a valued and reliable employ - ee who was simply having a bad day. Rather than reprimand her or make her feel worse about her predicament, Jim could try to ease her ten - sion through humor.

If he ignores the situation, she might lower others' morale by commu - nicating abruptly and harshly with them, the way she did with the intern. By helping Anne, he also helps the people who interact with her.

The best option is to help her lighten up and get over her bad mood.

Humor can take many forms, but the goal is to evoke pleasant feelings through unexpected or exaggerated acts of encouragement.

Based on her late arrival, it's likely Anne didn't have time for breakfast. Jim could go to a nearby deli and find something which would boost her energy, as well as her spirits.

The scenario might go something like this:

Jim places a lemon on Anne's desk and says, "This day's been a real lemon for you. I'm sorry it's been so rough, but you need to reboot."

With that, Jim could pull a bottle of lemonade from a bag and set it on her desk. Hopefully, Anne will start to laugh, breaking the tension as she begins to realize the world won't come to an end over one bad day.

After that, Jim could hand her a sandwich and a bag of chips, then encourage her to take a brief break in the lunchroom in order to regroup. After she's eaten, she can get a fresh start on the day.

A truly loving leader employs humor to lighten the mood and assist employees in being healthy and productive.

chapter nine

INTEGRITY
Begin Every Action With a Commitment to Integrity

Horrendous corporate scandals have plagued America the past few years, putting a spotlight on many companies' lack of integrity. Those breaches in ethics have caused the public to lose confidence, trust and respect for corporate leaders, something which has created a good share of angst in boardrooms, especially for those who have always done business in an honest way.

Only a handful of corporate leaders have been accused, indicted and convicted of corporate malfeasance, but, by association, their actions have tainted many other executives who had nothing to do with the scandals.

A large segment of society has concluded the typical corporate leader follows the Gordon Gekko philosophy of "greed is good." The same people tend to believe the pursuit of financial reward drives corporate leaders to do whatever it takes for the corporate compensation system to work in their favor, that their (potentially) short tenure as CEOs or senior executives will be richly rewarded for the substantial risk they take in assuming an unethical position.

Far too many CEOs face the prospect of a one- or two-year tenure and, consequently, arrange or negotiate terms of compensation which aren't in line with the quality of their performance.

Unfortunately for corporate America, the erosion of corporate integrity has created a burden for all leaders. Trust and mutual respect are fundamental to all relationships. It ensures enjoyable and efficient relationships and once that's lost, it's a huge challenge to regain it. Without trust, your interaction with customers, shareholders, associates and vendors is difficult to sustain. Time may heal the wounds, but scars will remain.

At the heart of trust is the commitment to integrity, which every individual in an organization has to have as a guiding beacon. Your conduct has to adhere at all times to the highest moral principles and professional standards. Truth, honesty and fairness aren't optional—they're mandatory. It may be challenging and occasionally unpleasant, but behaving with integrity is the only way to build trust in those who deal with you personally and professionally.

You have to build relationships founded on a commitment to integrity. Unfortunately, society's ethical standards have changed dramatically over the years. Under traditional mores, integrity was a core value. Those were the days when a handshake or verbal commitment would be honored.

Some believe the secularization of our society has diminished the impact of the religion-based moral and ethical standards which existed in America for centuries. The "absolute truth" standard seems now to have given way to the more nuanced view where answers aren't simply right or wrong, but much more "gray."

There are those in the corporate world who behave more like politicians—"spinning" or twisting the "truth," instead of being honest, but ethical executives still exist and outnumber the unethical ones. As a result of the corporate scandals, many organizations are now increasing efforts to improve their integrity, including adding ethics training for their employees.

What Is Integrity?

Maintaining a commitment to integrity in each and every one of your actions is a tough standard. So what is it exactly?

There are probably as many definitions of integrity as there are speakers and writers on the subject. In Webster's dictionary, integrity is defined as:

1. Firm adherence to a code of especially moral or artistic values: **incorruptibility**

2. An unimpaired condition: **soundness**

3. The quality or state of being complete or undivided: **completeness**

Integrity is doing the right and honest thing all the time—and always for the right reasons. High integrity behavior is sometimes easy, but doing the right thing can be difficult when the cost of an action appears to be greater than the benefit of maintaining integrity.

It's easy to tell the truth when the truth is already known, but it's much more difficult to answer a question truthfully when you know there's going to be a consequence coming back at you.

Integrity means you should always tell the truth—and not just when it feels good or is easy.

However, you may need to learn *how* to tell the truth.

If you tell your boss you slept in, rather than create a story about horrible traffic in the wake of a car accident, the truth could damage your career. You boss may think you have no discipline and can't wake up in time to get to work. The truth may set you free, but in this case, that freedom could be the loss of your job. A commitment to integrity might mean telling your boss the truth in a way which explains the mitigating circumstances which caused you to oversleep.

Telling the truth, or what's perceived to be the truth, is important, but the motivation shouldn't be self-serving.

For instance, if it's true a rival for your next promotion is a liar, to say that because you want to destroy his or her career isn't an action based in integrity. The right reason matters. Can you tell the truth in a way which doesn't destroy the person, particularly if it was a one-time mistake and completely out of character for the individual?

During a discussion on leadership and integrity at the Wharton Business School in April 2005, American Express chairman and CEO Kenneth I. Chenault described integrity as the single most important attribute and principle of leadership.

"Today, the stakes are incredibly high," Chenault said. "The need for leaders to stand for something and act from principle is more important than ever. Things that were acceptable five or ten years ago will today cost you your career… if you are not clear on who you are, on what it is you stand for, and if you don't have strong values, you are going to run your career off a cliff."[37]

Chenault said integrity is more than being honest, which is only a piece of it. He said it means being consistent in words and actions. Without strong values and actions consistent with those values, a leader won't succeed.

Some argue one breach of a leader's integrity can destroy any trust associates might have, while others argue it's only if there's an ongoing pattern of bad behavior which determines how someone is perceived. Still others find it difficult to accept any breach of integrity.

Chenault believes there is redemption for a few missteps.

"If your people believe that you have the right values, they will tolerate a few mistakes. In fact, they will stay with you," continued Chenault. "They want to see that you are decisive and compassionate, because you are asking people to take risks, to take chances. But don't confuse compassion with a reluctance to act decisively when necessary."[38]

Be Honest and Ethical With Your Employees

Love demands the truth. You have to exercise your commitment to integrity if you're going to be effective in your application of love during virtually every interaction your have with your employees.

However, you have to balance your commitment to integrity with your commitment to love. That means don't tell substantially less than the "whole truth" just because you want to avoid jeopardizing the psychological well-being of one of your associates. Yes, truth can be painful for all those involved.

How many times have you provided feedback to an individual and found the conversation more stressful than it would have been if you'd only remained silent? If you've had this sort of experience, you may try to avoid difficult conversations like that in the future, but if you do, you'll fail to effectively lead (and love) your associates.

You can't mask the full, candid and potentially hurtful truth in the guise of caring and sensitivity when you're communicating with your employees. That kind of caring isn't love. Instead, it often stems from your own fear the truth will have painful consequences—to you.

Fear can influence your willingness to be candid or direct with your associates during discussions about their performance. You may fear reprisal from a worker or you may be concerned even if they do have legitimate reasons to question, doubt or even aggressively challenge the accuracy of your observations.

You have to have the highest standards of integrity to understand your obligation to your organization and, irrespective of your fears, commit to taking high integrity actions.

If an associate doesn't receive your honest feedback, whether positive or negative, the result is he or she will be filled with anxiety rather than love. The loving thing to do is to be honest, but provide helpful feedback which encourages your employees to find ways to improve their performance or behaviors.

Your entire organization can suffer if you fail to have candid, direct and meaningful conversations with your associates. But, remember, a candid counseling session only has meaning when the "candor" is expressed with love. Candor without love can be brutal and hurtful.

Ultimately, you're the one accountable for the quality of your unit's performance. When you fail to provide meaningful feedback which is of the highest integrity, your organization is cheated of the potential for improved performance. Excellence can't be achieved without the commitment to continually improve each individual's performance because organizational performance reflects the sum total of individual performers in your organization.

A Culture of Integrity?

Have you ever worked for an organization which had values you thought were flawed? What did you do? Did you stay and just ignore the circumstances? Did you quit? This is a tough issue and there are no easy answers.

People hold different views about life and office politics. Political conservatives believe in the primacy of the individual and individual initiative. Liberals value the use of society to support the weak individuals collectively. These two positions set up potential conflict for any individual who might have a view of society which differs from the one currently in power.

Which side is right and which side is wrong?

Our philosophy on values and the core concepts of right and wrong may differ, but each of us in the workplace will eventually be faced with situations which require value-based decisions. There will be times when your personal values appear to conflict with your organization's values. When they do, you'll inevitably be faced with the need to reconcile conflict, resolve it, ignore it or walk away from it.

However, you don't need an untruth to create an integrity problem. A simple disconnect between the values of an organization and those of the individual can result in an integrity violation.

Let's say you believe your organization isn't honoring its customers. You see how your company always charges the highest price the market will bear, but, on a personal level, you believe customers should get the best service at the best price. How do you reconcile the organization's behavior with your own value?

In this case, a classical economist could easily conclude the organization has a core value of profit maximization, with an obligation to its shareholders to charge the highest price the market will bear. The behavior of charging the highest price is consistent with a core value of the enterprise, even though it violates your own personal sense of values. An organization with this profit maximization goal would probably believe anybody not working toward maximizing shareholder profit would be committing a breach of integrity.

The irony is many organizations don't have a clear expression of their values and, consequently, their employees or prospective employees have no way of knowing if the corporation's values conflict with their own personal values.

As an individual with a set of values, it's imperative you understand as much as possible about your organization's values before you join it. If there's a wide disparity, it will cause you great conflict and pain which could be difficult for you to resolve.

If you have a strong commitment to a value which is inconsistent with your organization's values, it may actually be a personal violation of integrity for you to remain in the organization. The organization also would probably be better off if all those who didn't subscribe to its values were to leave.

Any employee who doesn't behave consistently within the value structure probably will be viewed as creating an integrity breach.

Be Committed to Integrity
Can you have a commitment to integrity even if your organization

Work Leader's Tip: Values Threats

Here are some tips on determining what to do in a situation which challenges your values:

- It may seem obvious, but when faced with a question of fact, always tell the truth. That means, if somebody asks you to outright lie, don't—no matter what the rationale.
- When faced with a question about a colleague at work, avoid value judgments about his or her behavior or personality. The best way to avoid a dishonest or a "short on integrity answer" about your associates is to simply say, "We shouldn't gossip or talk about people." It doesn't mean you shouldn't have an opinion, but it does mean you should keep those kinds of opinions to yourself. The benefit is you won't hurt anybody and you're not forced to say nice things you don't honestly believe.
- Be candid, but not cruel. It's possible to be critical without hurting a person or an organization. When giving leadership feedback, think how you'd react to the same feedback.
- Never knowingly go to work for an organization which has low standards of integrity or ethics. If you discover a weakness, get a new job. Cultures with low standards of integrity and ethics always become hostile to those who choose to live by a higher standard.
- Never tolerate a breach of integrity in your own behavior. It's imperative to set the standard for your staff. Never accept the concept of following the "tone at the top."
- Never tolerate breaches of integrity in your organization. Set a high standard of expectations and hold those who fail fully accountable. You may choose to forgive, but you should never ignore misdeeds. Your staff needs to know you'll not tolerate a failure to behave ethically. Punishment may not be appropriate, but clear and unambiguous "corrective action" has to be taken.
- Avoid the temptation to compromise on core values just because it's convenient.

doesn't? Yes! Your behavior doesn't have to be controlled by anyone else but you.

You're responsible for your level of commitment to integrity, so if you believe in a set of values, then you can and should do what you believe to be right, irrespective of your organization's views. If you really believe, then you won't be distracted from your path.

In theory, your individual beliefs should dictate your behavior, but you're probably influenced by the "tone at the top." Top leadership establishes the norm of behavior which becomes the norm within the organization. The senior leaders of an organization may not realize it, but their impact on others is enormously powerful.

The culture at the top of the former energy commodities firm Enron appeared to be one which said, "Do the deal, no matter what the cost," and that adversely influenced many in that organization to act unethically. In 2001, the same year the company went bankrupt, an investigation revealed the company had made its fortune based on a well-planned accounting fraud. Some of Enron's top executives were convicted and sent to prison.

Eventually, corporate bad guys do get caught, but their actions still taint all corporations in the public's eyes.

What can you do if you're in a similar situation at your organization? What if you don't believe in the "kill for the deal" culture? Can there be a "sub-culture" which says, "Not all deals are worth doing if they harm others"?

Realize the corrosive nature of some organizations may make it virtually impossible for you to survive without acquiescing to the organization's values. Your company's leaders may have established a system which only rewards unethical behavior. If they value "cutthroat competition," that's the behavior they'll reward and the behavior the majority of employees will give them. Any "rogue" ideas by members of your organization will be driven out.

Let's go back to the question: can you value integrity when your organization doesn't? Yes, but not for long.

If you behave in a way which is inconsistent with the acceptable behavior, eventually one of three things will happen: 1) you'll change your behavior to conform to the "company standard" and become one of them; 2) you'll quit, with or without another job; or 3) you'll be fired.

The highly pessimistic reality is the Law of Bad Leadership will kick in: bad leaders at the top will drive out good leaders at the bottom. Eventually, the organization will end up with only those who sell out to a lack of integrity or those who never had any in the first place.

Is There Hope for High Integrity Leaders?

Don't be discouraged if you're in an organization where a lack of integrity appears to be the standard operating procedure. Continue to have a strong commitment to integrity because it's possible you can change your organization from within.

Yes, companies can change.

Many organizations have found a way out of a crisis because leaders, either from within or without, have committed to change. Unfortunately, some of that shift only comes about as a result of a crisis, usually following the public revelation of a major breach of ethics. But sometimes, if an organization's crisis is severe enough, it can cause the remaining board members, executives and employees to be shocked into a dramatic change. However, for that to take place, it's important for the cancer of lost integrity to not be so pervasive that only the weak or flawed are left in the company.

One example of an organization which lost its way is Hewlett-Packard. HP had very high standards and a rich culture of commit-

---

Work Leader's Tip: Are You Honest with Yourself?

Answer these questions honestly. Do you:

- Really love your job?
- Feel personally fulfilled?
- Feel proud of yourself and your achievements?
- Consider yourself successful in the things which matter most to you?
- Meet your own expectations? Exceed them?
- Meet your boss's expectations? Exceed them?
- Nurture your own personal needs and pursue your passions?

ment to a value system known as the "HP Way." Then chairwoman Patricia Dunn, in an effort to find an information leak, hired outside security experts to investigate her board of directors, along with several journalists, including those from the *Wall Street Journal* and the *New York Times.*

The security people Dunn hired then turned around and hired private investigators, who decided to use the illegal practice called "pretexting." The investigators, in an effort to find the "leak," fraudulently posed as board members and journalists in order to obtain other people's phone records.

The tragic story of HP's "fall from grace" demonstrates how a breach at the top can pollute an organization known for its virtuous business ethics. The scandal which ensued caused many to leave the board and HP. Several individuals, including Dunn, were indicted in California. Ultimately, it was discovered one of the board members had been the source of the information leak.

The good news was a strong ethical culture still existed deep inside HP and many honest employees started working with the new leadership to save the company. The integrity of those employees eventually prevailed and, ultimately, even caused the departure of a CEO for reasons of "inappropriate behavior."

When an unethical culture at the top leads to an organization's failure, integrity in employees and leaders lower down the hierarchical pyramid can have a positive influence and even resurrect a company. Good leaders at the bottom can overcome bad leaders at the top—invalidating the Law of Bad Leadership.

True, an organization's size, complexity and geographic dispersion may make it difficult to restore integrity, but there are countless examples which prove it's not impossible if only the top executives are corrupt, rather than the entire organization.

Some organizations manage to mask their lack of integrity for a surprisingly long time. The Enron story is a perfect example. Enron had been the darling of the investment community for decades and it took a financial crisis to bring the house of cards down.

In the case of another corporate ethic breach, this time at the then-second-largest long distance company WorldCom, it took the courage of an internal auditor to speak up and tell the Board Audit Committee she thought there was "something wrong" with the accounting.

Neither En ron nor WorldCom survived their executives' indictments and the ensuing corporate scandals.

The good leaders from within have to be an organization's salvation and cause others to commit to the value of integrity.

There Are Good Leaders and There Is Hope

One leader who exemplifies high integrity is Jon M. Huntsman. He started his company Huntsman Container Corporation in 1970 and within thirty years the company had become the largest privately-held petrochemical and plastics business in the world. Huntsman is widely recognized for his excellence in leadership, as well as his philanthropy, and has been honored with numerous awards.

When his company went public in 2005, it had annual revenues in excess of $12 billion and operations in forty-four countries. That same year, he wrote the book *Winners Never Cheat: Everyday Values We Learned as Children (But May Have Forgotten)*.

Huntsman's story demonstrates how success and integrity go hand-in-hand. The book is based on his personal business experiences, which serve as a moral compass for other leaders.

He advocates tough business negotiations, but insists they "must be fair and honest...treating customers, colleagues, employees and competitors with respect...Character is most defined by integrity and courage. Your reputation is how others perceive you. Character is how you act when no one is watching. These traits, or lack thereof, are the foundation for life's moral decisions. Once dishonesty is introduced, distrust becomes the hallmark of future dealings or associations."[39]

Huntsman also writes, "Compete fiercely and fairly—but no cutting in line. Which rules we honor and which we ignore determine personal character, and it is character that determines how closely we will allow our value system to affect our lives...Once you compromise your values by agreeing to bribes or payoffs, it is difficult ever to reestablish your reputation or credibility. Therefore, carefully choose your partners, be they individuals, companies or nations."[40]

Hire Ethical Employees

The advice to choose carefully is particularly relevant when evaluating the integrity of a potential employee. It's not an easy task. Uncovering an individual's true character can take time. How can you determine if someone has high standards of integrity when you only spend a couple hours in interviews with them?

There are several steps you can take to ensure you attract and hire people committed to integrity. First, it begins with your own behavior. Act with integrity in all your activities and you'll gain a reputation as someone who has excellent moral and ethical character. That kind of reputation will attract others who share your high standards.

Next, if your organization doesn't already have a statement of values and ethics, suggest one be created. This statement should define the behavior and ethics critical to your organization's culture of integrity. Each employee should have a printed copy of the statement and it should be posted on your company's website to demonstrate to potential customers and employees your company's commitment to integrity.

In the interview process, your organization's statement of values and ethics can be handed to candidates as a way of initiating a discussion of how important integrity is in your organization. Candidates who don't share those beliefs are likely to be uncomfortable and may realize the job isn't the right fit.

Another tactic for assessing character is to ask behavior-related questions, such as how they've handled difficult problems or customers. You could also ask the candidates to give examples of goals they've set and how they went about accomplishing them.

When you're ready to offer someone a job, take the time to verify the accuracy of the person's résumé and make sure you check their references. Ask their previous employers about the person's responsibilities, contributions, attitude and interaction with others. Some references will be more forthcoming than others, but, hopefully, you'll learn enough to support your sense the candidate has high ethical standards and will fit into your organization's culture.

Look for Ethical Employers

If you're the one looking for a new job, it's important for you to determine if your potential employers are really committed to integrity. That can be challenging.

Start by carefully researching organizations where you'd like to work. Read their websites thoroughly and check for position statements. Do an online search for news items and press releases which shed light on their social responsibility, financial practices and internal culture. Gauge the organization's reputation by talking to others who work in the same industry or have been clients or customers.

During an interview, ask questions which illuminate aspects of integrity, such as whether there's a code of ethics and what the organization's priorities are.

If you receive a job offer, you should ask to speak to others who can confirm your belief this is an organization with high standards of integrity. Your goal is to join a company where every individual believes in the value of integrity and behaves accordingly.

It's also important for you to find integrity mentors. Those mentors can be at the senior level, as well as at a relatively low level in an organization's structure. The goal is to form relationships with individuals whom you admire for their ethical and moral behavior. When faced with a difficult situation which requires you to make a value-based decision, you won't have to depend solely on your own ethics and morals. The advice of your mentors will support or challenge your sense of the right thing to do. By sharing the burden of ensuring integrity, you'll also strengthen the culture of commitment to integrity. To succeed as a leader, always remember success and integrity go hand-in-hand.

No matter what, make sure you maintain a commitment to integrity. It may seem, at times, an impossible challenge to live up to, but always do the right thing, no matter how tempting it is to compromise your values of right and wrong. You'll need to have that strong foundation of values because I guarantee you will be strongly tested with "real world" challenges.

Be Honest with Yourself

Integrity is the single most important attribute of leadership. If you don't have it, people you work with won't trust, admire, rely on or respect you. You'll never be "great" in the minds of those who have sound moral and ethical values, no matter what you accomplish in life or how many apparent successes you rack up.

Are you fair, honest and loyal?

If you were taught personal integrity when you were young, it's probably ingrained within your character and isn't something you have to work on or improve each day. In fact, you probably take it for granted. When others challenge you or put you into situations which require an integrity-based decision, you don't have to take the time to consider what adheres to your own values.

If your personal adherence to integrity is sound, you probably instinctively act ethical at work and don't have to give much thought to making "right" decisions which are honest and fair. It's likely your moral compass guides you and doesn't require serious attention, except in times when you're faced with an ethical crisis which might have been brought on by the behavior or decisions of others.

Personal integrity includes not just how you interact with others, but also how you interact with yourself. Only when you're honest and loyal to yourself will you be able to fulfill your greatness.

When did you last seriously think about whether you're personally fulfilled and what you can do to help yourself reach or maintain that feeling? Are you setting personal goals and are you achieving them? What matters most to you in life and are you nurturing it?

Case Study: Martha Forgets Integrity

Martha is the vice president of operations at a start-up technology com- pany headquartered in Silicon Valley, a position she's held for about ten months.

Before this job, she held similar positions in two other software start- ups. One turned out to be a success, but the other was a complete bust. Much of the latter experience was very unpleasant and the experience left scars which still haven't fully heal.

Martha invested a good deal of her own money into the second com- pany and within eighteen months, it closed its doors. Adding insult to injury, she discovered the company's CEO had lied to virtually every investor about the state of the company and was a fraud who'd squan- dered most of the cash which the venture capital firms had invested.

Martha was devastated by the experience and swore she'd never again make that mistake again. To guarantee that, she researched the princi- ples in her current firm before accepting her position and spent a good deal of time talking to people who'd worked with and for the current CEO. Martha's conclusion was that he was of the highest integrity.

She put her full energy into her job. She hired many of the same peo- ple who had worked for her at the previous "failed firm" and felt she'd assembled a great team. The company had a vision similar to her last company's, so it was easy for her to be excited and to recruit those who had been great employees at the previous company.

But over the last three months, Martha has developed serious reser-vations about her current CEO. There were subtle (but, to her mind, clear) signs he was making expenditures on wasteful and self-serving trips, equipment and even what she saw as personal "lifestyle perks." She wasn't in a position to be monitoring expense patterns, but she was con-vinced money was misused in a way which reminded her of what she'd seen in the last company.

Martha knew the CFO of her company pretty well and about a month ago decided to mention her concerns to him. After her conversa-tion (which she pleaded he keep confidential), she had an uneasy feeling the CFO wasn't very receptive to her anxiety. Her fears were then quick-ly confirmed when she was called into the office of the CEO and con-fronted with her "allegations." The meeting was pretty heated and by the time it was over, she found herself "repenting" and apologizing to the CEO for even the hint of distrust.

Since that meeting, her relationship with the CEO has clearly changed and Martha now finds herself distanced from much of the core decision making. Even worse, she's had several more experiences which reinforced her concerns the CEO wasn't being an effective steward of the investors' money. She's now concluded the situation will damage the com-pany, but she feels terribly unsure and conflicted as to what her next step should be.

Martha is at a crossroads. What should she do?

She has every reason to feel conflicted. There's an overwhelmingly strong case for spending improprieties. One the other hand, her previous experience has made her understandably "gun shy" about the warning signs she sees. It's not clear she has enough evidence to go forward with an allegation of impropriety or fraud.

What is clear is she has very few options. She can either: 1) not do anything, stay in her job and ignore the problem; 2) find another job and resign; 3) stay and continue to monitor the behavior of the CEO, even conduct her own investigation; 4) report her findings to one or more members of the board of directors and/or investors.

The first option is unfortunately the one many people take. This is tragic because it means the individual has essentially "condoned" the behavior, as well as sacrificed his or her individual sense of integrity. You shouldn't support that action because it's one of the reasons so many past corporation scandals went unchecked. Too many times, employees knew something was wrong, but they didn't do anything about it.

The second option is clearly a possibility. It would be easy to under-stand if Martha decided the best course of action for her would be to move on before the company "blows up." If the environment at the com-pany makes her uncomfortable, then an action to eliminate discomfort is reasonable. In this case, Martha tried to alert the financial control point and failed to produce a reasonable result.

The third action, or some version of it, is probably the one most peo-ple would opt for in the short-term. Assessing whether there's "evidence" of malfeasance is a reasonable course. The challenge for Martha is that her work climate is now tense, so she may find it difficult to obtain doc-umented "facts" which could be used to report the improprieties. It's also a challenge to determine where she should report the facts in the event she actually uncovers evidence.

The last action is theoretically the correct action, but it's fraught with risk. If Martha turns to any of the directors and investors and they in turn break her confidence as the CFO did, then there's little hope for her to have a career in the organization. On the other hand, if she does report it and they honor the request, then the truth might be determined by independent actions of the board and/or investors.

What would you advise Martha?

She could do several things in sequence. First, she should stay and continue to monitor, because what she's reported thus far is mostly anec-dotal and conjecture. It's advisable for her to try to find clear evidence, one way or the other. She should also begin to evaluate alternative job opportunities.

The relationship with her CEO has become noticeably strained, so she might want to move on, as it may not be possible for him to get past what he views as a breach of trust. Remember, if Martha is wrong about her fears, then she's wrongfully accused her boss. It's hard to get past that.

Finally, she should hold open the option of going to the board/investor group. Should she find concrete evidence, or another job, she should probably attempt to alert those people quickly.

Personally, my sense of integrity wouldn't allow me to just quit and walk away. I'd feel an obligation to alert somebody there might be a problem. If this were a public company, the securities regulations would require there be a "hotline" to which potential "whistle blowers" could provide their thoughts. I'm the chairman of the audit committee of sev - eral companies and, in each instance, we have a system to allow people to come forward with these kinds of suspicions.

chapter ten

PASSION
The Way to Drive Purpose and Performance

You'd better have passion if you're going to be a great leader. Passion is a driving force in the human spirit and when it's present, success is attainable. It creates purpose so you can overcome every challenge in your path. It also stimulates energy, desire, confidence and faith in your ability to achieve extraordinary results. Passion fuels your determination to overcome obstacles and cements your conviction you can complete whatever task you have to do. That kind of enthusiasm is a powerfully compelling emotion.

Passion is something you feel deep inside you which propels you forward and won't let anything stop you from pursuing and achieving your goals. In order to achieve sustained winning performance, you have to have the passion to achieve outstanding performance.

To understand how passion affects your behavior, consider reading a book you love versus one you don't. Some books you'll pick up and not be able to put down until you finish, while others will take you weeks to read—and you may never get to the end. The difference is the emotional commitment you feel—or don't feel—for each one.

The same is true for an assignment at work. If you love doing a task, you'll finish it quickly and do a better job than if it's an assignment you dislike or merely tolerate. Passion is what makes you committed to getting the results you want, whether it's making a personal relationship last, winning a competition or achieving greatness on the job.

An extraordinary performance almost always requires an extra expenditure or energy. To excel on the job, you may need to study, put in longer hours, learn something new (possibly something you don't find interesting), travel or sacrifice personal time for work. But, if you believe in the big picture and have passion for what you're doing, you'll be able to get through the less enjoyable parts with a minimum of pain.

If you don't have passion for your job, you'll be miserable and, ultimately, you won't succeed. If you just "get by" or survive, you won't live up to your own potential and you won't inspire your associates to live up to their potential either. Employees inevitably reflect the attitudes of their employers, so your passion, or lack of it, has an enormous impact on your staff.

In sports, you can see how passion impacts the outcome in almost every game. True, the players' natural capabilities, knowledge and skills contribute to the success or failure of most teams, but emotional passion drives the end result of competition much more.

Most of the teams in the National Football League (NFL) or the National Basketball Association (NBA) have players who are pretty comparable in terms of their skills. There are a few exceptions, such as the phenomenal quarterbacks Brett Favre and Peyton Manning, basketball giants Shaquille O'Neal, Michael Jordan and Labron James, but, by and large, on any given day, any team could win.

It's the ones with passion who will move ahead and achieve victory over others with the exact same skills.

The obvious differentiator is the role of emotion, which usually increases the amount of adrenaline flowing. Coaches encourage this by "pumping up" their teams with emotional speeches. The players then sustain that emotion with screams and enthusiastic celebrations of their every success. Their emotions may stem from anger at the foe, anger at the prospect of losing, fear of the coach's anger, or even excitement at the prospect of winning, but when the team is "pumped up," they often win, regardless of their skill level. It's not always the better team that wins, but rather the team which has the highest emotional investment.

Passion plays the same type of role in the world of work that adrenaline plays in sports. It creates a "high" which is exciting and makes you feel enthusiastic, energetic and upbeat. When passion is missing, there's a corollary "low" which may manifest itself as lethargy or apathy.

Once you experience the positive feelings which come with passion, you'll crave more. It becomes addictive, just like adrenaline. That means if you aren't passionate about your work, you're not going to be getting those positive feelings you crave. If that's the case, I suggest you start looking for another job where you can tap into your passion.

If you're not passionate about your job, consider whether it's the work itself or the organization. When you can identify what makes you want to perform and what holds you back, you'll be closer to finding a job which connects with your passion.

Passion Is Power

When you're really passionate about your work, that becomes an incredibly powerful tool for success. It's more than just wanting to win. When you're passionate about your organization's mission, as well as your leadership role and responsibilities, you'll be driven to perform in an exceptional way which exceeds your organization's goals and achieves what seems impossible.

But your passion has to be genuine. It can't be faked. Either you're fired up and enthusiastic about something, or you're not. You won't be able to influence or inspire your associates without a personal conviction in what you're trying to achieve.

If you view leadership as an assignment imposed on you by the parameters of your job, as opposed to a calling to enable others to achieve greatness, you're in the wrong job. Leadership is about helping others realize their extraordinary potential. It's not about giving the best speeches or receiving the most recognition from your superiors. It's about you uniting your team in a commitment to achieve superior results both for themselves as individuals and the organization as a whole.

Leaders are "people who leave their footprints in their areas of passion," wrote Dr. Jonathan Byrnes, a business consultant, in a 2005 article for his alma mater Harvard Business School.[41]

Not only is this an incredibly poetic way to describe leadership, it also captures the essence of how monumentally influential a leader can be. You should make all your employees feel their contributions make a difference and that their work has meaning.

"The 'meaning' is essential to the happiness of an individual, whether they are working for a large corporation, volunteering for a non-profit, or developing their own business," writes motivational leadership consultant Michele Payn-Knoper in a June 16, 2000 article titled *Passion: The Light of Leadership*. "After all, humans naturally

---

Work Leader's Tip: Ask These Questions to Clarify Your Self Focus

- Do you know anybody who's been passed over for a promotion? What happened to that person? Have you ever been passed over for a promotion you wanted? Why did that happen?
- If you answered "no" to the question above, how do you know you didn't lose a promotion without even knowing you were being considered? Sometimes you never find out about an opportunity for promotion.
- If you've been in your current job for five years or more, is there anything you should be doing to prepare for your next job? Has the organization given you any hints about what you should do?
- If you've been in your job for less than a couple of years, does the company have a plan for you? Does it fit your expectations? If it does, are you ready to move to the next job? If not, what do you need to do to get ready?
- Have you done a Strengths, Weaknesses, Opportunities and Threats (SWOT) analysis on yourself? If not, prepare the analysis, then ask yourself what you've learned. Show the analysis to somebody whose judgment you trust and ask that person to evaluate it.
- What's your long-term goal? Where do you want your life to be in ten years? In twenty years? Is there a match between your life goals and the career track you're on? If there's a divergence, what can you do to bring these two together?
- What are you going to do tomorrow to help you achieve your goals for the next year? What about next week? Develop a list of at least ten action plans for next week.

desire to make a positive contribution to society; a lasting impact on both the present and future. I believe great leaders recognize that need, draw upon it, and use it to engage individuals in your cause. Essentially, they draw others to the flame of your passion."[42]

As a Work Leader, you should be the torch-bearer for passion as an example to your employees. The brighter your flame, the more likely your associates will be drawn to it and follow it. Using passion to influence and lead your associates can be inspiring.

Because passion is so powerful, you must use it responsibly. Make sure it and the resulting power are channeled toward worthy goals. Passion can accomplish great good in helping mankind—or it can be the cause of great evil when it's misdirected. A good example of that is those who orchestrated the attacks on America on September 11, 2001.

Wielding the power of passion to simply satisfy your ego or to achieve self-serving goals is wrong and defies everything discussed in the previous chapter about integrity.

Recognizing Passion

The beauty of passion is everyone can have it. Just combine your personal talents, interests and motivation and you'll have it.

Far too many people aren't thriving at work because they suffer from a lack of passion. When your employees have passion for their work, their motivation will come from within. They'll require less supervision, perform better than those lacking it and can more easily be groomed to become leaders themselves.

When it comes to hiring individuals, passion is undeniably one of the prerequisites. You need to hire people with the appropriate skills, but it's also important to assess whether their interests and talents intersect with your organization's core mission, vision and goals. There's no formula for identifying whether potential hires have a level of passion which will mesh with your organization, but there are a few things to consider when you interview them.

First, after you identify what their individual talents are, find out if they understand what they really want to do, as opposed to simply naming what they've done in previous jobs. Have they sought out work in a field or position which matches their personal interests? If they lack the drive or initiative to seek out employment ensuring their own happiness on the job, they're not likely to have the drive to help your organization succeed in its mission.

"When you engage in work that taps your talent and fuels your passion—that rises out of a great need in the world that you feel drawn by conscience to meet—therein lies your voice, your calling,

Work Leader's Tip: Do These Apply to You?

If your answer to many of these questions is "no," then perhaps you need to consider whether there's a different job or organization where you could be more passionate.

- Do you gladly go to work early or stay late in order to excel?
- Do you frequently review your expectations and goals to make sure you're on track to meet them—and then beat them?
- Are you motivated more by the pleasure of your work than by the amount of your paycheck?
- Do you seek out ways to create enthusiasm and drive in your coworkers?
- Would your coworkers describe you as dedicated to your organization and its bottom line?
- Do you really believe in the organization's mission and goals?
- Do you love most aspects of your work?
- Are you optimistic you can achieve the goals are set for you, even if they're a big step above the status quo?
- Do you spend some of your free time doing things such as reading or networking in order to enhance or improve your job performance?
- Is this your dream job?

These questions aren't easy and require you to be honest with yourself. If you're not passionate about your work, you're lacking a key ingredient for success. Since success is the reward for hard work, it makes sense to find a job which brings out your passion.

your soul's code," wrote leadership guru Stephen Covey in *The 8th Habit: From Effectiveness To Greatness.*[43]

Using Passion to Inspire

Passion, like integrity, needs to be present from the top all the way down to the bottom of an organization. A positive spirit and attitude at the top will infuse the organization with energy and inspire enthusiasm. It also inspires loyalty and confidence. If your associates don't see passion in you or the head of your company, they won't feel passionately about your organization's mission.

Use your passion to help your employees ignite their own so they can exceed your expectations, even in the most challenging times. You have to inspire your workers so they feel motivated to love their job as much as you do. Note that you're to *inspire* them, not *control* them.

"When people think that someone else is in control of them then they don't have much passion," said Lindly "Bud" Mingledorff, chairman of the board of a large heating, ventilation and air conditioning company based in Atlanta, Georgia. "You have to teach people that their jobs are how they perceive it. They teach you in kung fu that competition is within you. What you're doing is you're competing with your inner self to become your very best. And if you can become passionate about that then how can you not be passionate about your job because it is you."[44]

Passion for work can take a variety of forms and means different things to different people. Some have that level of enthusiasm about their job and the challenge to perform their best, while others are passionate about their organization's mission and the outcome which results from their work.

One of my colleagues learned this lesson early in her career. After working for a boutique public relations firm which represented only a handful of clients in the film industry, she was hired as an account manager for a large, full-service PR firm. The firm's clients included a wide variety of businesses and individuals seeking to promote themselves through positive publicity and recognition in the media.

She soon discovered that working for so many diverse clients didn't appeal to her because she didn't believe in all of their messages or even their value to the public. Her lack of a passionate belief in her clients made her work unpleasant and she struggled to perform her best on their behalf.

A coworker of hers was the exact opposite. He was thrilled with each new challenge to create publicity and garner media coverage, regardless of who or what was being publicized. As a result, he became extremely good at his job, while my friend suffered through her responsibilities.

Miserable, my friend started looking for another job and soon found one heading up the in-house PR department for a company whose mission she did appreciate. There she started enjoying her work and felt personally invested in the organization's success.

She learned an important lesson about herself and the way in which passion plays a role in her personality and her desire to perform. Finding a job with a company she believed in and which made her feel passionate about her work was the right move. If she'd stayed in her former job where she wasn't genuinely enthusiastic about her work, she wouldn't have achieved any kind of success for herself or her organization.

Everyone has to find a job which triggers his or her passion to perform. But another big factor you have to consider is talent. Passion will carry you far, but you still need ability. You can't go higher than your skill level.

You may have a tremendous passion for tennis, but if you don't have the highly trained skills of someone playing on the professional circuit, you can't compete on their level. As much as you love tennis and are passionate about it, you're never going to be as good as a professional player who's also passionate, but far more talented in the sport. You have to have both passion and ability if you're going to be world class.

Find your talent and set a fire under it with your passion.

It would be wonderful if everyone who read this book would become passionate in their jobs and have associates who share that motivation, but, realistically, that won't be the case. Too many people merely show up for work, punch in and go through the motions, with no enthusiasm or emotional commitment.

As a leader, it's important for you to see signs and continually gauge the passion levels in your employees. Who's chronically late? Who never sacrifices a break, lunch or vacation for work? Who's consistently punctual and willing to stay late? Who's excited by opportunities for advancement and personal growth?

The associates who demonstrate passion are your potential stars, so ongoing development is your primary leadership responsibility to them. You also have to make sure they stay motivated. If a typically passionate associate begins to show signs of apathy and a lack of enthusiasm or commitment, you need to notice that and investigate where the problem lies.

Individuals who don't demonstrate passion won't serve themselves, you or the organization to the best of their abilities. Perhaps they're misfits in the work assignments or don't fit in the organizational environment. Whatever the case, it's your responsibility to help ignite their passion, either in the position working with you or at another job which would better utilize their talents. Ensuring your employees "buy in" to your company's vision with a passionate commitment is critical to everyone's success.

You won't be able to motivate everyone. If you don't succeed, encourage those workers to explore their passions on their own. Perhaps there's a different position for them in your organization or they might need to look elsewhere for a new job which fulfills them more than the one at your company.

Every employee needs to feel a personal passion, not only for his or her job, but also the organization as a whole. They have to strongly believe in their company's mission and its products, services and employees. When employees are that motivated, they'll help spread their passion throughout your company. That's because passion can be very contagious.

A life full of passion is colorful, exciting, exhilarating and fulfilling. Without it, life is dull, boring, uninspiring and lackluster.

Help your employees ignite their inner passion so they'll have more fulfilling lives.

Passion Is Potential

Passion inspires purpose, power and potential. Only with passion will you have the unwavering conviction that what you're trying to achieve is possible. It gives you the confidence to reach for your goals, no matter how ambitious or far-reaching. It unleashes your potential and infuses you with the courage and conviction to achieve extraordinary things.

You won't feel passion every second of every day any more than you can run full-steam on adrenaline all the time. Just make sure you have enough passion to counteract the difficult, challenging times when you have to persevere.

A young associate of mine once told me about a leader who had a lasting, positive impact on his life. It was his fifth grade teacher, a passionate educator who taught this young man to challenge himself. He discovered not only were those challenges really rewarding, but also that hard work and discipline gave him a lot of self-satisfaction, with the potential for even better things.

He learned some tasks or activities are exciting, while others are more tedious and a person's attitude and perspective are their personal choice.

When a student would complain about something being "boring," the teacher and the other students would thump their hands rhythmically on their desks and chant in unison, "Boring people are easily bored."

Work and personal responsibilities are full of chores which can't be avoided, whether you find them exciting or not. Certainly it's in your best interests to engage in work and personal activities which coincide with your individual passions, but there are always going to be mundane parts of your life which are necessary, too. Just make sure your passion is strong enough to see you through those periods. See past them for the potential of even greater things.

If you discover you're generally feeling lackluster and unenthused at work or in your personal life, remember, you have a choice: you can either decide to be bored, or choose to have a life full of energy and excitement.

Assess which areas of your life seem to be fulfilling and which areas are missing passion. Determine what you want and what really excites you, then pursue it. Although it may require some soul searching, you can identify something you care deeply about, something which really excites you and you want to achieve. The things which spark your passion are actually the easiest to incorporate into your life because you'll have the drive, determination and faith to make them happen.

That's the potential of passion.

Only when you consistently nurture yourself will you be able to fully and selflessly give your best to your associates. If you lack the passion to lead, lack passion for your job or fail to incorporate passion into your life, you won't reach your full potential as a leader or even as a person.

If you make the promise to yourself to always seek and embrace passion as an essential aspect of your life and to apply all of leadership principles to yourself, success and personal fulfillment are yours for the taking.

Case Study

Charlie and Jane lived in Chicago and had been married for two years. They were both passionate about their careers and that passion had translated into their success and promotions.

Jane was the executive chef of a small restaurant which had gained local acclaim for creative gourmet cuisine. She'd begun to receive personal recognition after a journalist from a national gourmet magazine visited the restaurant and wrote a complimentary review. Her goals to run the kitchen at a big-name restaurant and, ultimately, open her own restaurant were proceeding according to her plan.

Charlie had started his career as a sales representative for a textile company. He really enjoyed his work and was extremely loyal to his company because the upper management had consistently treated him well and rewarded his successes. The year he and Jane got married, he exceeded his sales goals by 100 percent. In addition to financial bonuses, his company awarded him a week-long vacation in Jamaica which enabled him to treat his wife to a wonderful honeymoon. Following that banner year, he was promoted to Midwest regional sales manager and continued to shine in his performance.

Five months ago, Charlie was invited to a meeting at the corporate headquarters and was given another opportunity for a promotion. He was asked to become the operations manager of the company's plant in a small town in South Carolina. The chance to advance his career to the next level was thrilling to Charlie, but the relocation and lifestyle changes were issues.

He knew the move would impact Jane's career and be a challenge for her on a personal level because all of her family and friends lived close by.

The two debated the pros and cons of the move and within a month had made the firm decision for Charlie to accept the promotion. Jane was crushed she'd have to leave the job she loved so much, but she was determined to make the best of it for her husband's benefit. She felt it would be unfair to hold him back in his career and he'd had a long history with his company.

Furthermore, Charlie's income far exceeded Jane's and they wanted to put money aside so they could start a family. Even if the pay was less for her, she was sure she could easily start over at a different restaurant and eventually open her own.

Charlie is now thriving in his new position in South Carolina. His leadership skills have enabled him to improve productivity at the plant, which has had a favorable impact on the company's revenue. He quickly developed a good rapport with his staff and initiated new employee reward programs, which boosted morale and made him a popular new face in the community.

However, Jane is having the opposite experience.

There are no gourmet restaurants in town, so the only job she could find was the head cook at a restaurant which is part of a national chain. She has no chance to use her own recipes or creativity and the kitchen and wait staff appear to go through the motions with little regard for quality and service.

The fact Jane is miserable and dreads going to work is obvious to Charlie. He suggested she quit working at the restaurant, but that only sparked an argument—and arguments have become increasingly common since their move.

"Staying home alone all day while you're at work won't make me happy and we need the second income," said Jane. "Even if we could put practicality aside, I miss the gratification of using my talent to create wonderful meals. Not to mention the fun of working with people who are equally excited to please customers and provide a memorable dining experience."

Should Jane quit her job? If so, then what?

Unfortunately, whether for financial or personal reasons, people sometimes end up in jobs for which they have no passion.

When you find yourself in this situation, it's time to start looking for a new job immediately. If you lack passion for your work, you won't perform well and you won't achieve any kind of success. There's also the very real possibility that if you don't quit yourself, you'll probably be fired *because your performance won't match your company's expectations. However difficult it may seem to overcome the obstacles and challenges which arise from finances or family obligations, you owe it to yourself to find a solution.*

Passion isn't an optional part of your work equation—you have to have it in order to achieve success.

In Jane's case, she's so unhappy in her job, it could destroy her emotional well-being and possibly her marriage.

First, she needs to take a step back and make an honest assessment of why she's so unhappy. Is it just a result of the constraints imposed by cooking for a chain restaurant and the staff's apathy? Or is she being unfair and viewing the staff harshly because they're small-town folk with different ways than metropolitan city workers?

If she can really assimilate into the town's lifestyle and community, then she should have many options for work and a chance to fulfill her passion.

Since the town lacks a gourmet restaurant, she could explore the option of opening her own where she could train her staff to work according to her standards and expectations. The food and format would likely be different from what's popular in Chicago, but designing a restaurant and menu which would appeal to the locals would be a creative challenge for her.

Another option would be to start a catering business for weddings and special events.

She could also reinvent herself to some degree and start a cooking school, or compile her recipes into a cookbook, which she could promote and sell online.

She could open a restaurant consulting business and travel to various towns and cities in the area. That way she could help train other chefs and their staffs.

She might come up with her own product line of home-cooked specialty items and sell them at farmers' markets and town fairs.

There are numerous options for Jane to pursue her passion and she needs to start looking for the right situation as soon as possible.

LEADERSHIP
Love to Passion Revisited

Our journey began with understanding the role of love in setting the tone of the relationship with your associates and concluded with a focus on making sure passion is a part of your life.

Between committing to honing your capacity to love associates and the role of loving and leading yourself, you have to set expectations, make a correct assignment, focus on development, provide effective evaluation, deliver timely rewards, implement systems, embrace humor, honor integrity and pursue passion. These leadership practices are necessary to foster, encourage and assure peak performance from your associates. However, the real intensity of your efforts has to be on yourself.

The role of Work Leader places a burden on you which can't be treated lightly. When you were an individual performer, your capacity to deliver results was the true measure of your success. As a leader, you'll probably continue to do tasks which generate results for your organization, but your true measure of success shifts dramatically. Now you have to help your associates achieve success as individuals and as a team.

You're not leading the work—you're leading your employees. Your duty as a Work Leader is to love your associates enough to make sure you expect, assign, develop, evaluate and reward them and their performance on the job. But you also have to lead yourself. In the same way you make sure your associates fulfill their potential, make sure you, also, develop yourself and fulfill your potential.

But your greatest happiness should come from the success of others. Realize your success and happiness come from being part of a team. As a Work Leader, your only avenue to success is for your unit to succeed. Having a staff to lead means the organization believes more than one associate is required to achieve the unit goals. That's why you can't achieve success all by yourself. Your staff's pain of failure or excitement at success has to be yours. Your goal has to be to help staff members stay focused on the goals because their achievements will be your achievement.

The most effective way for your associates to grow and succeed is to learn from you. You're the bright beacon guiding them to achieve. The ten concepts outlined in this book are fairly simple, but the actual tasks of being a leader is tough work. Just as you needed to be trained to do your previous work assignment as an individual performer, you now have to develop the skills of a Work Leader.

Although most organizations recognize the challenge, few have discovered the secret of developing peak performance Work Leaders. All too often, Work Leaders are "thrown into the water" to sink or swim with no real swimming lessons. Most tend to "doggy paddle," but never learn to swim. They simply learn to avoid drowning. Are you one of those?

If so, teach yourself to swim with these ten essential steps for success. Then, pass on your knowledge, skills and attitudes to your associates. The reason is simple: somebody in your unit will probably one day be asked to step into your shoes as a leader.

You owe it to all your associates to help your successor be more ready than you were.

ACKNOWLEDGMENTS

This book is the result of thousands of hours of working with leaders of organizations of a wide range of size, complexity and type. I've worked with leaders from Fortune 50 companies, privately held companies, closely held public companies, large and small not-for-profits and even the boards of companies where I was the principal shareholder.

In addition, I've served many organizations in many leadership capacities and my colleagues in those organizations continue to help me develop in my understanding.

Each of these experiences has enriched my understanding and I've grown immeasurably by those interactions. I owe each of them a huge debt of gratitude for helping me to better comprehend how leaders can change the course of their organizations

The writing of this book started at the beginning of my managerial career when I was teaching first-line supervisors about managing. Those days in the classroom helped to shape my views of what leadership was all about and I learned from every student and subordinate I worked with or taught. As I moved through the managerial ranks, every one of the hundreds of Work Leaders I knew influenced my thinking and my leadership skills. I owe them all for helping me through my successes and my failures to lead them well.

This book has had the benefit of scores of people who have reviewed a broad range of drafts of the manuscript. My heartfelt thanks to Dave Heenan, Jerry Porras, George Rieder, Karen Street, Jean Folwell, Ken Gould, Dick Buxton, Doreen Tyburski, Ann Vessels, Julie Swano, Elizabeth Bassett, Kim Stoneberger, Robyn Lighthammer and countless supervisors. They offered candid, even sometimes painful, feedback—all beneficial.

This book is built on the foundation of knowledge my mentor Gail Melick gave me. He shaped much of my thinking on leadership and I've continued to feel the impact of his guidance throughout my career. He became the most influential person in my professional development, someone who always inspired me with his warmth, discipline and unwavering commitment to excellence with the impact of his mentoring continuing throughout my career.

I owe a significant thank you to every manager and supervisor in the subsidiary companies of the Deltennium Corporation who suffered through reading early drafts and who ultimately helped me make the book more meaningful.

I owe a huge debt to my original editor, Sharon Goldinger, who saved me from myself. Her discipline and attention to detail had a huge impact on whatever quality the book has. She took a raw manuscript and helped me make it something which communicated efficiently what I wanted to say. Whatever is good about this book exists because she found a way to make a rank amateur look better. She helped me to learn and, if I ever write another book, she'll help me start with a better work product.

I also owe a huge debt to Barbara Bendall, who was the editor on this second edition. Barb helped me to integrate the new chapters, and even forced me to become less formal and more conversational. I think she's right—the book feels more natural.

I'm also enormously grateful to my wonderful wife Lois. She suffered through several drafts of almost every chapter as it was created. Her honest feedback many times forced me to go back and rethink the book, while her attention to detail helped minimize the serious grammar and punctuation errors. This book is a testament to her patience.

Gerald M. Czarnecki
Boca Raton, Florida
July 1, 2014

ENDNOTES

1 John William Gardner, *On Leadership* (New York: The Free Press, Inc., 1990), 3-4.

2 Joe D. Batten, *Tough-Minded Leadership* (New York: American Management Association, 1989), 2.

3 James C. Collins and Jerry I. Porras, *Built to Last: Successful Habits of Visionary Companies* (New York: Harper Collins, 1994), 213.

4 John P. Kotter, *On What Leaders Really Do* (Boston: Harvard Business Review Book, 1999), 16.

5 John C. Maxwell, *The Twenty-One Irrefutable Laws of Leadership: Follow them and People Will Follow You,* (Nashville: Thomas Nelson, 1998), 101.

6 Allan J. Cox, *The Making of The Achiever* (New York: Dodd, Meade, 1985), 12.

7 Warren G. Bennis, *On Becoming a Leader* (Reading: Addison-Wesley, 1989).

8 John William Gardner, *On Leadership* (New York: The Free Press, Inc., 1990), 1.

9 Beverly A. Potter, *Changing Performance on the Job* (New York: American Management Associations Publications Group, 1980), 67.

10 Thomas Gordon, *Leader Effectiveness Training* (Solana Beach: Wyden Books, 1977), 20.

11 Norman R. Augustine, *Augustine's Law* (New York: Viking Penguin, 1983, 1986), 363.

12 Joe D. Batten, *Tough-Minded Leadership* (New York: American Management Association, 1989), 142.

13 Nicolo Machiavelli, *The Prince* (New York: The New American Library of World Literature, 1952), 49.

14 James C. Collins, *Good to Great; Why Some Companies Make the Leap...and Others Don't* (New York: Harper Collins, 2001), 41.

15 Henry Mintzberg, *The Structuring of Organizations* (Englewood Cliffs: Prentice Hall, 1979), 83.

16 Richard A. Fear, *The Evaluation Interview* (New York: McGraw-Hill, 1978), 12.

17 Andrew S. Grove, *High Output Management* (New York: Random House, 1983), 203.

18 Jay W. Lorsch and Thomas J. Tierney, *Aligning the Stars* (Boston: Harvard Business School Press, 2002), 2.

19 Stephen R. Covey, *Principle-Centered Leadership* (New York: Simon and Schuster, 1992), 246.

20 Harry Levinson, *The Exceptional Executive, A Psychological Conception* (London: Oxford University Press, 1968, 1970), 133.

21 Thomas Gordon, *Leader Effectiveness Training* (Solana Beach: Wyden Books, 1977), 8.

22 Kenneth Blanchard, Patricia Zigarmi and Drea Zigarmi, *Leadership and the One Minute Manager* (New York: Blanchard Management Corporation, 1985), 53.

23 Marcus Buckingham and Curt Coffman, *First, Break All the Rules: What the World's Greatest Managers Do Differently* (New York: Simon and Schuster, 1999), 57.

24 Douglas McGregor, *The Human Side of Enterprise* (New York: McGraw-Hill, 1978), 87.

25 Andrew S. Grove, *High Output Management* (New York: Random House, 1983), 188.

26 Norman R. Augustine, *Augustine's Law* (New York: Viking Penguin, 1983, 1986), 364.

27 Saul W. Gellerman, *Management By Motivation* (New York: American Management Association, 1968), 23.

28 Justin Fox, "What Ben Franklin Can Teach Execs." *Fortune* (March 9, 2006), retrieved from http://http://money.cnn.com/2006/03/08/magazines/fortune/pluggedin_fortune/.

29 Benjamin Franklin, *The Autobiography of Benjamin Franklin* (In public domain).

30 Ann Fry, *Laughing Matters: The Value of Humor in the Workplace* (Amazon.com Books).

31 Andrew Bridge, "Ten Ways to Motivate the Next Generation of Workers," *Globe and Mail*, (November 16, 2012), retrieved from http://www.theglobeandmail.com/report-on-business/small-business/sb-tools/top-tens/ten-ways-to-motivate-the-next-generation-of-workers/article5085339/.

32 Herb Kelleher, CNBC interview, retrieved from http://www.cnbc.com/id/100000634.

33 Matt Weinstein, *Managing to Have Fun: How Fun at Work Can: Motivate Your Employees, Inspire Your Coworkers, Boost Your Bottom Line* (New York: A Fireside Book, 1996).

34 David Granirer, "Using Humor at Work," retrieved from www.granirer.com/ART-0005.htm.

35 Matt Weinstein, *Managing to Have Fun: How Fun at Work Can: Motivate Your Employees, Inspire Your Coworkers, Boost Your Bottom Line* (New York: A Fireside Book, 1996).

36 Roger von Oech, *A Whack on the Side of the Head: How You Can Be More Creative* (New York: Time Warner Books Group, 1998).

37 Kenneth I. Chenault, "AmEx's Ken Chenault Talks about Leadership, Integrity and the Credit Card Business," lecture at the University of Pennsylvania's Wharton Business School, *Knowledge@Wharton* (April 20, 2005), retrieved from http://knowledge.wharton.upenn.edu/article/amexs-ken-chenault-talks-about-leadership-integrity-and-the-credit-card-business/.

38 Kenneth I. Chenault, "AmEx's Ken Chenault Talks about Leadership, Integrity and the Credit Card Business," lecture at the University of Pennsylvania's Wharton Business School *Knowledge@Wharton* (April 20, 2005), retrieved from http://knowledge.wharton.upenn.edu/article/amexs-ken-chenault-talks-about-leadership-integrity-and-the-credit-card-business/.

39 Jon M. Huntsman, *Winners Never Cheat: Everyday Values We Learned as Children (But May Have Forgotten)* (Pearson Prentice Hall, 2005).

40 Jon M. Huntsman, *Winners Never Cheat: Everyday Values We Learned as Children (But May Have Forgotten)* (Pearson Prentice Hall, 2005).

41 Dr. Jonathan Byrnes, "The Essence of Leadership," Harvard Business School *Working Knowledge* (September 6, 2005), retrieved from http://hbswk.hbs.edu/archive/4983.html.

42 Michele Payn-Knoper, "Passion: The Light of Leadership" (June 16, 2000), retrieved from http://www.causematters.com/articles/passion-the-light-of-leadership/.

43 Stephen Covey, *The 8th Habit: From Effectiveness To Greatness* (Free Press, 2005).

44 Lindly "Bud" Mingledorff, "CEO's Speak on Leadership: Vision and Passion," *Executive Evolution*, retrieved from http://www.executiveevolution.com/Leadership_Vision.htm.

BIBLIOGRAPHY

Allen, Louis A. *Making Managerial Planning More Effective* (New York: McGraw-Hill, 1982).

Augustine, Norman R. *Augustine's Law* (New York: Viking Penguin, 1983, 1986).

Batten, Joe D. *Tough-Minded Leadership* (New York: American Management Association, 1989).

Bennis, Warren and David A. Heenan. *Co-Leaders* (New York: John Wiley and Sons, 1999).

Bennis, Warren G. *On Becoming a Leader* (Reading: AddisonWesley, 1989).

Blanchard, Kenneth; Zigarmi, Patricia; and Zigarmi, Drea. *Leadership and the One Minute Manager* (New York: Blanchard Management Corporation, 1985).

Bossidy, Larry and Ram Charan. *Execution* (New York: Crown Business, 2002).

Buckingham, Marcus and Coffman, Curtis. *First, Break All the Rules: What the World's Greatest Managers Do Differently* (New York: Simon and Schuster, 1999).

Byham, William C., PhD. *Zapp! The Lightning of Empowerment* (New York: Harmony Books, 1988).

Champy, James. *Reengineering Management* (New York: Harper Collins, 1995).

Clavell, James. *The Art of War by Sun Tzu* (New York: Delacorte Press, 1983).

Collins, James C. *Good to Great; Why Some Companies Make the Leap...and Others Don't* (New York: Harper Collins, 2001).

Collins, James C. and Porras, Jerry I. *Built to Last: Successful Habits of Visionary Companies* (New York: Harper Collins, 1994).

Connellan, Thomas K. *How to Improve Human Performance* (New York: Harper and Row, 1978).

Conner, Daryl R. *Managing at the Speed of Change* (New York: Villard Books, 1993).

Covey, Stephen R. *Principle-Centered Leadership* (New York: Simon and Schuster, 1992).

Covey, Stephen R. *The 8th Habit: From Effectiveness To Greatness* (Free Press, 2005).

Cox, Allan J. *The Making of The Achiever* (New York: Dodd, Meade, 1985).

Crosby, Philip B. *Quality Is Free* (New York: McGraw-Hill, 1979).

DePree, Max. *Leadership Is an Art* (New York: Doubleday, 1989).

Drucker, Peter R. *Management: Tasks, Responsibilities and Practices* (New York: Harper and Row, 1973).

Fear, Richard A. *The Evaluation Interview* (New York: McGraw-Hill, 1978).

Franklin, Benjamin. *The Autobiography of Benjamin Franklin* (In public domain).

Fry, Ann. *Laughing Matters: The Value of Humor in the Workplace* (Amazon.com Books).

Gardner, John William. *On Leadership* (New York: The Free Press, Inc., 1990).

Gellerman, Saul W. *Management By Motivation* (New York: American Management Association, 1968).

Goldratt, Eliyahu M. *The Goal* (Croton-on-the Hudson: North River Press, 1992).

Gordon, Thomas. *Leader Effectiveness Training* (Solana Beach: Wyden Books, 1977).

Grove, Andrew S. *High Output Management* (New York: Random House, 1983).

Harry, Mikel and Schroeder, Richard. *Six Sigma* (New York: Doubleday, 2000).

Heenan, David A. *Double Lives: Crafting Your Life of Work and Passion for Untold Success* (Palo Alto: Davies-Black, 2002).

Huntsman, Jon M. *Winners Never Cheat: Everyday Values We Learned as Children (But May Have Forgotten)* (Pearson Prentice Hall, 2005).

Imai, Masaaki. *Kaizen* (New York: Random House Business Division, 1986).

Jick, Todd D.; Kanter, Rosabeth Moss; and Stein, Barry A. *The Challenge of Organizational Change* (New York: The Free Press, 1992).

Johnson, Harold E. *Mentoring for Exceptional Performance* (Glendale: Griffin Publishing Group, 1997).

Johnson, Spencer, MD. *Who Moved My Cheese?* (New York: G.P. Putnam's Sons, 1998).

Kanter, Rosabeth Moss. *The Change Masters* (New York: Simon and Schuster, 1983).

Kotter, John P. *On What Leaders Really Do* (Boston: Harvard Business Review Book, 1999).

Kotter, John P. *The Leadership Factor* (New York: The Free Press, 1988).

Levinson, Harry. *The Exceptional Executive, A Psychological Conception* (London: Oxford University Press, 1968, 1970).

Levinson, Harry. *The Great Jackass Fallacy* (Boston: Division of Research Graduate School of Business Administration Harvard University, 1973).

Lorsch, Jay W. and Tierney, Thomas J. *Aligning the Stars* (Boston: Harvard Business School Press, 2002).

Machiavelli, Nicolo. *The Prince* (New York: The New American Library of World Literature, 1952).

Maxwell, John C. *The Twenty-One Irrefutable Laws of Leadership: Follow them and People Will Follow You*, (Nashville: Thomas Nelson, 1998).

McConkey, Dale D. *How to Manage by Results* (New York: AMACOM, 1983).

McGregor, Douglas. *The Human Side of Enterprise* (New York: McGraw-Hill, 1978).

Mintzberg, Henry. *The Structuring of Organizations* (Englewood Cliffs: Prentice Hall, 1979).

Ogawa, Morimasa. *Pana Management* (Tokyo: PHP Institute, 1991).

O'Toole, James. *Vanguard Management* (Garden City, NY: Doubleday, 1985).

Ouchi, William G. *Theory Z* (New York: Avon Publishers, 1981).

Paulson, Terry L. *Making Humor Work* (Boston: Course Technology, 1989).

Peters, Thomas J. and Waterman, Robert H. *In Search of Excellence: Lessons from America's Best Run Companies* (New York: Harper and Row, 1981).

Peters, Tom. *Thriving on Chaos* (New York: Alfred A. Knopf, 1987).

Potter, Beverly A. *Changing Performance on the Job* (New York: American Management Associations Publications Group, 1980).

Senge, Peter M. *The Fifth Discipline: The Art and Practice of the Learning Organization* (New York: Doubleday, 1990).

Shorris, Earl. *The Oppressed Middle: Politics of Middle Management* (Garden City: Anchor Press/Doubleday, 1981).

Tichy, Noel M. and Stratford, Sherman. *Control Your Destiny or Someone Else Will* (New York: Currency Doubleday, 1993).

von Oech, Roger. *A Whack on the Side of the Head: How You Can Be More Creative* (New York: Time Warner Books Group, 1998).

Waterman, Robert H., Jr. *The Renewal Factor* (Toronto: Bantam Books, 1987).

Weinstein, Matt. *Managing to Have Fun: How Fun at Work Can: Motivate Your Employees, Inspire Your Coworkers, Boost Your Bottom Line* (New York: A Fireside Book, 1996).

Wheatley, Margaret J. *Leadership and the New Science* (San Francisco: Berrett-Koehler Publishers, 1992).

GERALD "GERRY" M. CZARNECKI

Gerald Czarnecki is Chairman and CEO, as well as the principal stockholder of The Deltennium Group, Inc., which has interests in a range of principle investments and is a broad consulting practice. The Deltennium Group helps organizations achieve peak performance through effective leadership, focused strategy, effective organization and sound financial management.

Mr. Czarnecki has conducted board of director governance seminars and in-board room consultancies on topics such as: managing audit committees; the board role in risk management and strategy; board and CEO evaluation; leading and managing the board dynamic; compensation practices; and financial skills for directors. A major focus of his attention is to help Work Leaders learn how to be effective in leading while they are doing, a challenge which all first line managers face everywhere.

Mr. Czarnecki is also Executive Producer and Chairman of Ventureland Productions, Inc., a full service Media and Marketing organization providing branded entertainment TV programming. Its latest programming was *The Suzanne Show*, staring Suzanne Somers and airing on Lifetime.

Mr. Czarnecki has written six books: *You're in Charge...What Now?*, a book focused on leadership for the work leader; *You're a Non-Profit Director...What Now?*, a primer on non-profit board governance best practices and *Success Principles for Leaders*, a book designed to supplement the core principles in his first book with specific insights into real world issues. His fourth book, *Lead with Love*, outlines ten principles every leader needs to maximize potential and achieve peak performance. He challenges all leaders to love their associates rather than simply like them and weaves that theme throughout the book. His fifth book, *Leadership is...Just One Things After Another*, is a collection of practical advice to leaders at every level about everyday issues. Mr. Czarnecki's sixth book, *Take Two, and Call me in the Morning, Prescription for a Leadership Headache*, offers a thirty-day program for dealing with predictable leadership challenges.

Prior to forming the Deltennium Group, Mr. Czarnecki was President of UNC Incorporated, a diversified aerospace and aviation company engaged in manufacturing, after market services and military outsourcing services. While at UNC, which had previously experienced serious performance losses, Mr. Czarnecki transformed the focus of a product and technology based organization to that of a customer oriented and service focused organization. His commitment to effective measurement of "value creation" for the shareholders, associates and customers was the basis of a redesigned management system premised on disciplined strategic marketing, continuously improving operations and customer centric management focused on creating shareholder value.

In 1993 Mr. Czarnecki was part of the team recruited by Louis Gerstner to begin the turnaround of IBM Corporation. Serving as a Senior Vice President in Human Resources and Administration, Mr. Czarnecki had worldwide responsibility for IBM's human resources, real estate services, quality programs, non manufacturing procurement, aviation and a wide range of other staff functions. Among his responsibilities was the management of the corporate-wide reengineering project which was targeted at the complete redesign of the business processes across all business units in what has become referred to as a "clean sheet" approach to systems and process reengineering. This effort required the coordination and project leadership across all research and development, manufacturing, marketing and distribution functions, as well as all staff support and information technology activities.

Prior to joining IBM, Mr. Czarnecki held a number of executive positions in the retail banking and consumer financial services industry, most recently as Chairman of the Board and CEO of Bank of America Hawaii.

In 1987 he joined an investor group headed by former U.S. Treasury Secretary William E. Simon and became Chairman, President and CEO of Honfed Bank in Honolulu. Honfed, a consumer bank, was one of many which had failed during the thrift crisis of the 1980's, but through Mr. Czarnecki's leadership and the substantial efforts of the partnership, the bank achieved superior levels of profitability through: successful market share increases; dramatic increases in total revenues; and dramatic decreases in overhead and other operating expenses. While Chairman of the bank, Mr. Czarnecki achieved enhanced growth of the retail customer base through the execution of mass retail merchandising techniques and an uncompromising commitment to customer service.

Recognizing the importance of community involvement to positioning the consumer bank, he also significantly enhanced the visibility of the consumer franchise through substantial personal commitments to community activities, resulting in his election to an unprecedented two terms as Chairman of the Hawaii State Chamber of Commerce.

Following Honfed Bank's sale to BankAmerica Corporation in 1992, Mr. Czarnecki continued as Chairman and CEO.

From 1984 to 1987 he served as President and CEO of Altus Bank, a Consumer and Mortgage Banking company. Altus had retail operations in banking, mortgage banking and had several subsidiaries, one of which was the largest residential housing developer in Mobile, Alabama, Pensacola, Florida and New Orleans, Louisiana.

From 1979 to 1982 Mr. Czarnecki was Executive Vice President of Finance and Administration at Republic Bank Houston. In 1982 he was appointed Senior Vice President of Finance at RepublicBank Corporation, becoming Executive Vice President of the company in 1983.

Between 1968 and 1979 he held various general management posts at Continental Bank of Chicago, eventually becoming deputy General Manager of the Trust and Investment Services department.

Mr. Czarnecki holds a B.S. in Economics from Temple University, an M.A. in Economics from Michigan State University, a Doctor of Humane Letters from National University and is a

Certified Public Accountant. He has been a frequent speaker at industry meetings, has written many journal articles on governance, leadership and general management and has been an adjunct professor at Depaul University, the University of Houston, Rice University, the University of Hawaii and Southern Methodist University.

He serves on several boards of directors, in some cases as a principal investor and in others as a fiduciary, independent director. He is a member of the Board of Directors of State Farm Insurance Company, Chairman of the Audit Committee and a member of the Corporate Executive Committee; as well as a member of the Board of Directors of State Farm Bank and State Farm Fire & Casualty.

Mr. Czarnecki is also Chairman of the Board of Directors of MAM Software Group, Inc. and is a member of the advisory board for Private Capital, Inc.

His nonprofit board positions include serving as member of the Board of Trustees of National University and is its former Chairman. He is a board member and member of the Executive Committee of JA Worldwide, Inc., is Chairman of the Compensation Committee, and is currently the Chairman of the CEO Search Committee.

From 2007 to 2008 Mr. Czarnecki was interim President and CEO of Junior Achievement Worldwide as the organization searched for a new CEO. He was also Chairman of the National Association of Corporate Directors - Florida Chapter.

In addition, he is Founder and Chairman of the Board of National Leadership Institute (NLI), a nonprofit organization dedication to facilitating quality leadership and governance in nonprofit organizations. The mission of NLI is to partner with educational institutions in order to facilitate the research, development and delivery of governance and leadership support for other nonprofit educational, social service and membership organizations.

Made in the USA
Las Vegas, NV
29 June 2022